DISCIPLE Makers

13 Fun Filled Bible Lessons About Following Jesus

Susan L. Lingo

Standard
PUBLISHING

CINCINNATI, OHIO

DEDICATION

**Therefore go and make disciples of all nations,
baptizing them in the name of the Father
and of the Son and of the Holy Spirit.
Matthew 28:19**

Disciple Makers
© 2000 Susan L. Lingo

Published by Standard Publishing, Cincinnati, Ohio
A division of Standex International Corporation

Credits

Produced by Susan L. Lingo, Bright Ideas Books™
Cover design by Diana Walters
Illustrated by Marilynn G. Barr and Megan E. Jeffery

09 08 07 06 05 04   7 6 5 4
ISBN 0-7847-1148-8
Printed in the United States of America

CONTENTS

INTRODUCTION

POWERING UP YOUR KIDS' FAITH!

Congratulations! You're about to embark on a wonderful mission to strengthen, energize, and stabilize your kids' faith and fundamental knowledge of God—faith and fundamentals that will launch your kids powerfully into the twenty-first century!

Disciple Makers is part of the Power Builders Series, an exciting and powerfully effective curriculum that includes *Value Seekers, Faith Finders, Servant Leaders,* and *Disciple Makers,* the book you're now holding.

Disciple Makers is dedicated to building and reinforcing kids' faith so they can serve and live in today's—and tomorrow's—world. Thirteen theme-oriented lessons will help your kids discover what it means to be a disciple of Jesus, understand why they want to be disciples, and explore how they can be Jesus' disciples every day of their lives. In addition, woven throughout each lesson is Scripture, Scripture, and more Scripture!

Each lesson in *Disciple Makers* has the following features:

POWER FOCUS (Approximate time: 10 minutes)—You'll begin with a mighty motivator to get kids thinking about the focus of the lesson. This may include an eye-popping devotion, a simple game, or another lively attention-getting tool. Included is interactive discussion and a brief overview of what kids will be learning during the lesson. *Purpose: To focus attention and cue kids in to what they'll be learning during the lesson.*

MIGHTY MESSAGE (Approximate time: 15 minutes)—This is the body of the lesson and includes engaging Bible passages that actively teach about the lesson's theme. The Mighty Message is not just "another Bible story," so your kids will discover God's truths through powerful passages and important portions of Scripture that are supported by additional verses and made relevant to kids' lives. Processing questions help kids explore each side of the passages and their relation to the theme, beginning with easier questions for young children and ending with more challenging think-about-it questions for older kids. Meaty and memorable, this lesson section will help kids learn tremendous truths! *Purpose: To teach powerful biblical truths and offer thought-provoking discussion in age-appropriate ways.*

MESSAGE IN MOTION (Approximate time: 10-15 minutes)—This section contains engaging activities that enrich and reinforce the lesson theme. It may include creative crafts, lively games and relays, action songs and rhythmic raps, mini service projects, and much more. *Purpose: To enrich learning in memorable and fun ways that build a sense of community.*

SUPER SCRIPTURE (Approximate time: 10-15 minutes)—This all-important section encourages and helps kids effectively learn, understand, and apply God's Word in their lives. The Mighty Memory Verse was chosen so every child can effectively learn it during the course of three weeks, but an extra-challenge verse is offered for older kids or children who can handle learning more verses. You are free to substitute your own choice of verses in this section, but please keep in mind that the activities, songs, crafts, and mnemonic devices are designed for the Mighty Memory Verse and the accompanying extra-challenge verse. And remember, when it comes to learning God's Word, effective learning takes place when kids work on only one or two verses over the course of several weeks! *Purpose: To memorize, learn, recall, and use God's Word.*

POWERFUL PROMISE (Approximate time: 5-10 minutes)—The lesson closes with a summary, a promise, and a prayer. You'll summarize the lesson, the Mighty Memory Verse, and the theme, then challenge kids to make a special commitment to God for the coming week. The commitments are theme-related and give kids a chance to put their faith into action. Finally, a brief prayer and responsive farewell blessing end the lesson. *Purpose: To make a commitment of faith to God and express thanks and praise to him.*

POWER PAGE! (Take-home paper)—Each lesson ends with a fun-to-do take-along page that encourages kids to keep the learning going at home. Scripture puzzles, crafts, recipes, games, Bible read-about-its, Mighty Memory Verse reinforcement, and more challenge kids through independent discovery and learning fun. *Purpose: To reinforce, review, and enrich the day's lesson and the Mighty Memory Verse.*

PLUS, in every Power Builder's book you'll discover these great features!

★ **WHIZ QUIZZES!** At the end of each section is a reproducible Whiz Quiz to gently, yet effectively, assess what has been learned. Completed by kids in about five minutes at the end of lessons 3, 6, 9, and 12, the Whiz Quiz is a nonthreatening and fun measuring tool to allow teachers, kids, and parents to actually see what has been learned in the prior weeks. When kids complete each Whiz Quiz, consider presenting them a collectible surprise such as a cool pencil and pad to symbolize that they are disciples (or learners) of Jesus. For example, after the first Whiz Quiz, present each child with a pencil case. After the next Whiz Quiz, present one or more pencils. Then use nifty erasers and cool notepads for lessons 9 and 12. When the book is complete, kids will have an entire "school" set to help them continue learning about being a disciple of Jesus. Kids will love the cool reminders of the lessons and their accomplishments! Be sure to keep children's completed Whiz Quiz pages in folders to present to kids at the end of the book or at the end of the year, in combination with other Whiz Quizzes from different books in the Power Builders Series.

★ **LESSON 13 REVIEW!** The last lesson in *Disciple Makers* is an important review of all that's been learned, applied, accomplished, and achieved during the past twelve weeks. Kids will love the lively review games, action songs, unique review tools, and celebratory feel of this special lesson!

★ **SCRIPTURE STRIPS!** At the back of the book, you'll discover every Mighty Memory Verse and extra-challenge verse that appears in *Disciple Makers*. These reproducible Scripture strips can be copied and cut apart to use over and over for crafts, games, cards, bookmarks, and other fun and fabulous "you-name-its"! Try gluing these strips to long Formica chips to make colorful, clattery key chains that double as super Scripture reviews!

★ **TEACHER FEATURE!** Discover timeless teaching tips and hints, hands-on help, and a whole lot more in this mini teacher workshop. Every book in the Power Builders series offers a unique Teacher Feature that helps leaders understand and teach through issues such as discipline, prayer, Scripture memory, and more. The Teacher Feature in *Disciple Makers* is "Prayer in the Classroom."

God bless you as you teach with patience, love, and this powerful resource to help launch kids into another century of love, learning, and serving God! More POWER to you!

PRAYER IN THE CLASSROOM

Ah, we teach our children so many wonderful things in our class-
rooms, from Scripture verses and Bible stories to God's truths and
how to apply them in our lives. But what about teaching prayer? *Teaching
prayer?* Hold on a minute! No one can teach prayer—you just *do* it, right?
Wrong! We need to teach prayer in our classes as much as we need to teach
any of the other wonderful things we work so hard to get through to kids!
Prayer isn't an innate activity or one that we're born "just doing" any more
than we're born reciting John 3:16 or the Ten Commandments. Yet prayer is
perhaps the most overlooked area for instruction in the history of the Christian
classroom! Let's explore a little about prayer and why it's essential to provide
at least some instruction for kids to understand and grasp the fullness of
prayer so they can make it a daily, lifelong habit.

"Lord, teach us to pray, just as John taught his disciples." So begins Luke
11:1 with the disciples' plea to Jesus to instruct them in the way of powerful
prayer. Even the disciples knew there must be something more to this intimate
time with God than first meets the eye. And just how did Jesus respond? Did
he turn them away saying, "Oh, there's no need for that! Just talk to God. It's
a natural thing, you know?" No, Jesus took the time to give his disciples a precious lesson about prayer—and us a dear passage of Scripture better known
as the Lord's Prayer. Jesus offered us important guidelines for praying to our
heavenly Father and encouraged his disciples to pray in that way. If the disciples recognized the need for prayer instruction and Jesus provided us a perfect prayer model, why isn't prayer a more studied area in children's Christian
education?

Have you ever invited your kids to pray aloud for the class? Chances are
you'll see more nervous glances than goodies at a bake sale! Reluctant kids
aren't against praying aloud any more than most adults receiving the same invi-
tation. Shyness, insecurity, and lack of words are usually the culprits keeping
our kids from the fullness of prayer and the wonderful gift of praying for others in God's presence. So let's discover a few practical ways to teach prayer

and to give our kids the encouragement and tools to offer sound, solid, spirit-filled prayer in a classroom setting and during their own private prayer times. For when kids have a prayer model and a bit of security, their voices will rise to the Father in beautiful prayers that still all heaven to hear!

PRAYER FINGERS

These simple fingers of prayer and faith will enable kids to see the importance of praying and help them begin to feel more comfortable praying for themselves and others. You may wish to make cool prayer gloves, labeling each finger as you learn what it means and what God promises with it. Or better yet, let kids make their own gloves and learn as you go and grow!

Finger 1—God commands us to pray. Help kids discover that prayer is commanded by God and not just something we do at church to end services. Jesus tells us to continue to pray when we feel hopeless (Luke 18:1), when we have troubles (James 5:13), and when we're in need (Matthew 7:7). We're to pray continually (1 Thessalonians 5:17) and in the spirit on all occasions (Ephesians 6:18). Knowing that prayer is commanded by God and done willingly by those who love him feels good to kids and helps ease some of the shyness in praying, especially in a group.

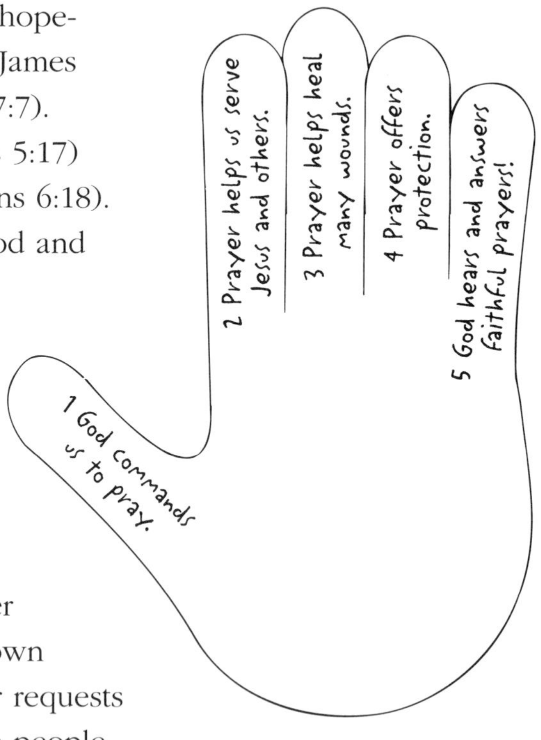

Finger 2—Prayer helps us serve Jesus and others. With immense love and passion, Jesus offered a moving prayer for his disciples, for himself, and for our own needs in John 17. Jesus didn't keep prayer requests for himself, nor did he only pray for those people whom he knew personally at that time. Jesus prayed for all the world and many millions of people who weren't even born yet! Jesus lifted intercessory prayers to God on our behalf out of love, servitude, and selfless giving. Helping kids understand that praying for others is a beautiful way to serve the Lord as well as others goes a long way in teaching them the power of prayer!

(hand illustration labeled:)
1 God commands us to pray.
2 Prayer helps us serve Jesus and others.
3 Prayer helps heal many wounds.
4 Prayer offers protection.
5 God hears and answers faithful prayers!

Finger 3—Prayer helps heal many wounds. Perhaps one of the most neglected powers of prayer is that of healing. Modern chemistry, prescription drugs, and a host of doctors may be needed to cure or alleviate illness, but the prayers of the faithful will do miraculous things! God is *Yahweh Ropheka,* our healer, and power to heal lies in his hands (Exodus 15:26; James 5:15, 16). Kids recognize suffering, whether it's their own or other people's afflictions, and kids realize that suffering can be as much physical as it is emotional. Teaching kids the power of healing prayer brings comfort, peace, and security because they know that health is in God's hands and will.

Finger 4—Prayer offers protection. The Bible tells us very clearly in several powerful passages that prayers offered to God for his protection and safekeeping are all-powerful and can drive away darkness! Jesus himself told Peter to pray against temptation (Matthew 26:41). Ephesians 6:16, 18 caution us to take up the shield of faith, which includes faithful prayer. James 4:7, 8 tell us to submit and to draw near to God in order to resist Satan. What better way is there to do this than through powerful prayer?

Finger 5—God hears and answers faithful prayers! What a stalwart truth to lean into and rely upon! God *does* hear our prayers and will answer in his time and in his way—God has promised us (Zechariah 13:9b)! What can be more powerful and secure for a child than to know that God *is* listening! "His ears are attentive to their prayer" (1 Peter 3:12). Help kids understand that God always has time to listen to and answer their prayers in his way.

When kids understand why we pray and what promises God makes to those who pray, a willing and more confident prayer attitude is inevitably born! Use the following ideas to help nurture prayer in your classroom and to begin kids on a lifetime journey of drawing near to God in powerful, sweet, comforting, and even commanding prayer.

ECHO PRAYERS—Before class, write a simple prayer that the entire class can pray. Write the prayer on newsprint for everyone to read, then read each line and have children echo back the words to the prayer. End with a corporate "amen." *Purpose: To give kids an example of praying; to help kids feel comfortable praying aloud.*

GOD-CAN PRAYERS—Let each child decorate a tin can with designs and the words "God Can If We Pray!" Provide slips of paper each week for kids to jot down a quick prayer. Then invite kids to read their prayers in small groups and deposit their requests in their God-Can containers. Have kids read through them often to see how and when God answers! *Purpose: To offer practice composing prayers; to encourage kids to look for how God answers their prayers.*

PRAYER PACKAGES—Hand kids colorful paper and let them write a prayer for a partner in class, then roll the prayer like a scroll and tie it with a bright ribbon. Tell kids to read their special prayers at bedtime, then offer their own prayers for the person who prayed for them. *Purpose: To teach children to pray for others in intercessory prayer.*

PRAYER LETTER HANDS—Use this hand as a pattern and enlarge it on poster board. Write the following, one on each finger: Greet God; Praise God; Needs & Wants; Praise God; Close Prayer. As kids sit in a prayer circle, pass the hand to five kids and have each pray according to a finger. For example, kids might say, "Dear heavenly Father [Greet God], You are all-powerful and loving [Praise God]. Please help us to be good disciples and to serve you and others every day [Needs & Wants]. Your examples of love are perfect and complete [Praise God]. In Jesus' name we pray, amen" [Close Prayer]. *Purpose: To give kids practice praying for and in a group; to give kids a simple prayer model.*

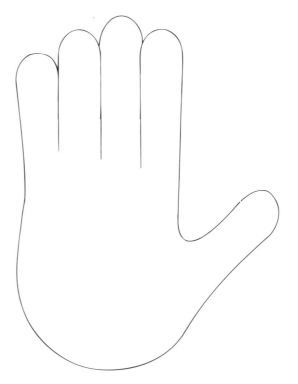

JESUS' BIRTH AND BOYHOOD

We have seen and testify
that the Father has sent
his Son to be the Savior of
the world.
1 John 4:14

GOD'S PERFECT PROMISE

Disciples have faith
in God's promises.

Isaiah 42:6, 7
Micah 5:2, 4, 5

SESSION SUPPLIES

★ Bibles

★ small boxes and gift wrap

★ bows and gift tags

★ scissors and tape

★ small nativity sets

★ permanent and regular
  markers

★ shoe-box size boxes

★ PVC pipe

★ twigs

★ construction paper

★ newsprint

★ photocopies of the Perfect
  Promises handout (page 123)

★ photocopies of 1 John 4:14
  (page 127)

★ photocopies of the Power
  Page! (page 19)

MIGHTY MEMORY VERSE

We have seen and testify that the Father has sent his Son
to be the Savior of the world. 1 John 4:14

SESSION OBJECTIVES

During this session, children will
★ discover what being a disciple is
★ understand that God keeps his promises
★ learn that disciples trust God's Word
★ realize that all things happen in God's time

BIBLE BACKGROUND

The dictionary defines a disciple as one who is taught by
the master and who assists in spreading the master's teach-
ings. What a perfect definition for those who are taught by
the one true Master, Jesus! But how many of us are disciples
in the fullest meaning of the word? Many who turn to Jesus
do become believers but leave their commitments at the
steps of the church and rarely put them into action. But to
be a disciple in the fullest sense involves *action:* active learning, active serving, active faith, and active involvement in
seeking Jesus.

Kids often have a hard time distinguishing between apos-
tles, disciples, followers, and believers. After all, if we love
Jesus, aren't we all of the above? Not necessarily! It's important to teach kids that being a disciple of Jesus takes more
than just words; it involves actively learning and imitating

Jesus. Use this lesson to help kids realize that the first thing a disciple learns is faith in God's Word and promises!

POWER FOCUS

Before class, purchase a small nativity set for each child. If you can't find the sets, you can make your own by purchasing several bags of small plastic farm animals and birds and putting two to three animals in each box along with several small figurines or wood cutouts of people (you'll need four plus a baby). If you really want a cute set, make a tiny manger by gluing dried grass to a paper-covered matchbox.

Place the nativity sets in small boxes, then wrap the boxes in festive gift wrap and bows and place gift tags with kids' names on the packages. Pile the gifts on a table for kids to see as they arrive.

Warmly greet kids and let them know you're glad they came. Then point out the colorful gifts and say: **Those are such pretty packages! What do you think could be inside?** Invite kids to tell their ideas, then ask:

★ **Why are gifts so wonderful?**

★ **How does it feel to wait for a special gift?**

★ **When someone gives you a special gift, what does it say about how that person feels toward you?**

Say: **Gifts are such fun, and some are valuable! When we have a promise of a special gift, it's often hard to wait until that gift arrives, isn't it? That's when we need real patience! A long time ago, God promised his people a special gift, but God didn't tell them when it would arrive.** Ask:

★ **How do you think the people felt about waiting for God's promise?**

★ **Why is it important to trust God's timing and to be patient?**

★ **How does having patience demonstrate our faith and trust?**

Say: **God always keeps his promises. That's why we can have faith that God will deliver his promises each and every time. We just need to be patient and let God decide when the time is right!**

I promise that you'll receive these gifts, too—but it's not quite time yet! It's hard to wait for wonderful surprises, but even God's people had to wait and have faith that God would keep his promise. Today we'll learn that God's special promise was for all of us and was a way for God to demonstrate his love for us. We'll discover that we need to have faith in God's promises even when it takes a lot of patience! And we'll begin learning a new Mighty Memory Verse that tells us who God sent as our Savior.

We'll also be discovering what a disciple is and what disciples do as we make cool Disciple Kits over the next several weeks. Right now, let's learn more about the wonderful promise God made to his people and to us as we discover what good detectives you are! Keep the gifts on the table. You'll give out the gifts during next week's Power Focus, but don't tell the kids yet.

THE MIGHTY MESSAGE

Before this activity, photocopy the Perfect Promises handout from page 123, one for each child. You'll also need a marker for each person. Have kids form several small groups and distribute the Perfect Promises handouts and markers. Say: **God knew long ago his people needed help to overcome mean people, disobedience, and sin. So God made a promise to send help to his people. And though God didn't tell his people just when the special gift would arrive, God did give them clues as to what the gift would be! As I read from the Bible, you can listen for clues to God's promise. When you think you hear a clue that tells something about God's promise or what his promise would be, gently wave your papers in the air.**

Read aloud the following verses. As kids wave their papers, have them tell what a verse says about Jesus as God's promise, then write the clues inside the heart shape on the handouts. Read Isaiah 42:6, 7:

★ **"I, the Lord, have called you in righteousness; I will take hold of your hand."** (Clue: God's promise will be righteous and guided by God.)

★ **"I will keep you and will make you to be a covenant for the people and a light for the Gentiles."** (Clue: God's promise is for all people, including the Gentiles.)

★ **"To open eyes that are blind, to free captives from prison and to release from the dungeon those who sit in darkness."** (Clue: God's promise will set captives free.)

Then read Micah 5:2, 4, 5:

★ **"But you, Bethlehem Ephrathah, though you are small among the clans of Judah, out of you will come for me one who will be ruler over**

POWER POINTERS

Photocopy the Disciple ID cards from page 123 on stiff paper. Let kids color and sign the cards. Cover the cards with clear adhesive paper. Have kids bring and "flash" their cards before each lesson!

Israel, whose origins are from old, from ancient times." (Clue: God's promise will come from Bethlehem and will be king.)

★ **"He will stand and shepherd his flock in the strength of the Lord, in the majesty of the name of the Lord his God."** (Clue: God's promise will lead his people in God's name and by his power.)

★ **"And they will live securely, for then his greatness will reach to the ends of the earth. And he will be their peace."** (Clue: God's promise will bring peace to people, and he will be praised all over the world.)

Have kids read the clues aloud. Then say: **Wow! God gave us many powerful clues to his special gift. Who do you think God was promising?** Pause for responses, then say: **When we read God's promises today, we know he was talking about Jesus. But long ago, God's people didn't know Jesus and could only trust and hope that God would send a savior to help them. But we know that God did send a Savior to love us and to forgive our sins. And as disciples, we have faith that God keeps his promises! Let's begin work on cool Disciple Kits that will teach us what being a disciple of Jesus is all about.** Save the Perfect Promises handouts to use later.

THE MESSAGE IN MOTION

Before class, saw a length of 2-inch PVC pipe into 6-inch segments, one for each child. PVC pipe can be purchased at hardware and building centers, or you can visit a building site and ask for any leftover pieces they may have. You'll also need a small twig and shoe-box sized box for each child.

Set out permanent markers, the boxes, construction paper, scissors, and tape. Hand each child a twig and a piece of PVC pipe. Say: **We can think of promises like these twigs. They're fine as long as they're whole. But what happens when they are broken?** Snap the twigs, then have kids try to put them together again. Say: **Once promises are broken, there's no way to put them together again. It's hard to trust human promises because they're too often broken. But God's promises aren't just stronger—they're unbreakable!** Have kids try to snap the pipes in half. Then continue: **God's promises are unbreakable, so as disciples, we can put our faith in them!** Ask:

★ **How is a disciple different from a friend?**
★ **How is a disciple different from someone who just believes in God?**
★ **How does Jesus teach us?**

★ How does being Jesus' disciples help us trust in God's promises?

★ What kinds of things do disciples learn?

Say: **During the next several weeks, we'll be exploring what being a disciple is all about and why being a disciple makes us powerful followers of Jesus. Each time we meet, we'll be adding another part to our Disciple Kits, and when we're finished you can take them home to teach others what being a disciple is all about. Today let's decorate our kits and pieces of PVC pipe.**

As kids decorate the boxes and PVC pipes, ask questions such as "How did Jesus' disciples learn about God?" and "What good things did Jesus' disciples do?" Point out that the PVC pipe can help us remember what God promised us with Jesus: **P**romised **V**ictory through **C**hrist. When the boxes are complete, have kids place their tubes inside. Then say: **The first pieces in our Disciple Kits remind us that God promised victory through Christ—or PVC. And we know that disciples have faith in God's promises! Next week we'll add another piece to our kits.**

We've learned that being a disciple means learning, and disciples know that learning God's Word is important because it contains special and powerful promises for us! Let's learn a new Mighty Memory Verse that teaches us more about one of God's special promises.

SUPER SCRIPTURE

Before class, photocopy the Scripture strip for 1 John 4:14 from page 127 for each child. Write 1 John 4:14 on a sheet of newsprint and tape it to the wall for kids to read. Keep this paper for kids to use for the next two weeks.

Gather kids in front of the verse on the wall and help them look up 1 John 4:14 in their Bibles. Read the verse from the Bible or from the paper on the wall. Read the verse three times aloud, then say: **What a powerful verse this is! It tells others that we have seen and can tell people that God sent Jesus to be our Savior.**

★ **How can we see Jesus?** (Help kids understand that we "see" Jesus through what he has taught and how we live as disciples.)

★ **What can we tell others about Jesus being our Savior?**

Say: **As disciples, we want others to know that Jesus is our Savior. And this verse says that we have seen and can tell others about our Savior! Here's a good way to remember this verse: we'll look for pairs.** Explain that the word *seen* has to do with our eyes (point to your eyes) and that the word *testify* has to do with our mouths (point to your mouth). Point out that *Father* (point upward) and *Son* (point upward again) go together and that *Savior* (make a cross with your fingers) and *world* (hold your arms in a circle) fit together because the world needed a Savior.

Repeat the verse two more times, using the motions. Then invite pairs of volunteers to repeat the verse using the hand motions.

We have seen and testify (Point to eyes and mouth.)

that the Father has sent his Son (Point upwards two times.)

to be the Savior of the world. (Make a finger cross, then an
arm circle.)

1 John 4:14

Say: **Remember, disciples are ones who learn from their leader. Jesus is our leader and wants us to learn God's Word. See if you can practice this verse twice a day for the next week to learn it well! Now let's add the Mighty Memory Verse to our Perfect Promises papers.** Have kids tape the Scripture strips for 1 John 4:14 under the hearts on their handouts.

Say: **We've learned that we can have faith in God's promises. Now let's make a promise of our own to God, then we'll share a prayer thanking him that we can be disciples of faith!**

A **POWERFUL** PROMISE

Before class, write the words to the disciple rhythm-rap in this activity on newsprint and tape it to the wall or a door for kids to see.

Have kids sit in a circle and hold their Perfect Promises papers. Ask for a moment of silence, then say: **We've learned today that a disciple is some-one who is a follower taught by a leader and that, as Jesus' disciples, we're taught by our perfect leader, Jesus. We've discovered that disciples have faith in God's Word and in God's promises. And we've started learning a new Mighty Memory Verse that teaches us that Jesus is our Savior. First John 4:14 says** (pause and encourage kids to repeat the verse with you), **"We have seen and testify that the Father has sent his Son to be the Savior of the world."**

Hold the Bible and say: **Because we know God is truthful, we trust him. And as disciples, we**

can trust God's promises because God never lies. He does what he says—all the time! Let's make our own special promises. We can say, **"I'll be a disciple who has faith in you, God."** Pass the Bible until everyone has had a chance to make a promise.

Then say: **Let's thank God for the perfect promises he made about the birth of Jesus. Let's go around the circle, and if you would like to read one of the promise clues on your paper, you may read it aloud. It's fine if we read a promise more than once. When we finish, we'll say "amen."**

Have children read the promises from Isaiah and Micah, then end with a corporate "amen." Have kids put their names at the bottoms of their papers to show they're disciples, then roll the papers like scrolls and place them inside the PVC pipes in their Disciple Kits.

Gather kids in front of the disciple rap you taped to the wall. Read the words in a snappy rhythm, then have kids tell what each line means. Remind kids that they can take pride in being Jesus' disciples, then have kids repeat the rap twice.

I'm not just a follower—that couldn't be much hollower!
I'm not just a sin-quitter, quiet Christian, pew-sitter!
I'M A DISCIPLE! A DISCIPLE OF JESUS!

I learn the lessons Jesus taught;
I know my life by him was bought;
Jesus is my every thought—
I'M A DISCIPLE! A DISCIPLE OF JESUS!

Say: **Being a disciple is very important. We have an important job to do, and that is to learn all we can about Jesus and then pass that learning on to others. As you go through this week, remember the first thing a disciple knows: A disciple has faith in God's promises—no matter how long he or she has to wait! Next week we'll open the wonderful promise packages we looked at today, so be sure to come! If you can't make it next week, don't worry; you can open your gift when you return because these promises, just like God's, are for everyone!**

End with this responsive good-bye:

Leader: **May you be a faithful disciple.**

Children: **And also you!**

Distribute the Power Page! take-home papers as kids are leaving. Thank children for coming and encourage them to keep their promises this week.

POWER PAGE!

Perfect Promise

God promised the birth of Jesus long before it happened. What clues did God give for his special promise?

a _ _ _ _ _ _ for the Gentiles
 3 (Isaiah 42:6)

He will be their _ _ _ _ _ _
(Micah 5:5) 1 2

a ruler over _ _ _ _ _ _ _
Micah 5:2 4 5

a covenant for the _ _ _ _ _ _
(Isaiah 42:6) 6

will come from _ _ _ _ _ _ _ _ _
(Micah 5:2) 7

What does God give away yet always keep?

His _ _ _ _ _ _ _ _ _ _ !
 1 5 6 7 3 4 2 4

THE FIRST DISCIPLES

Jesus chose 12 disciples. Use Matthew 10:2-4 to help you fill in their names.

1. Peter
2. Andrew
3. James
4. John
5. Philip
6. Bartholomew
7. Thomas
8. Matthew
9. James
10. Thadeous
11. Simon
12. Judas

High & LOW

Use 1 John 4:14 to help you fill in the missing high, low, and in-between letters.

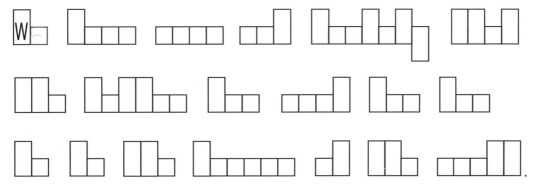

19

JESUS IS BORN!

**Disciples celebrate
Jesus!**

Luke 2:8-20

John 3:16

SESSION SUPPLIES

★ Bibles

★ gift boxes from last week

★ candles and matches (or
flashlights)

★ Christmas music

★ party blow-out horns

★ wide ribbon

★ Christmas cards

★ scissors and construction
paper

★ tape and fine-tipped markers

★ photocopies of the Power
Page! (page 27)

MIGHTY MEMORY VERSE

We have seen and testify that the Father has sent his Son
to be the Savior of the world. 1 John 4:14

*(For older kids, add in John 1:14a: "The Word became
flesh and made his dwelling among us.")*

SESSION OBJECTIVES

During this session, children will

★ discover that disciples celebrate and praise Jesus

★ learn that God kept his promise of sending a Savior

★ realize that disciples honor Jesus in many ways

★ offer thanks for God's greatest gift

BIBLE BACKGROUND

Who were the first disciples? Were they Andrew, Peter,
James, and John, as we're told in Matthew 4? Technically,
yes, but consider for a moment the shepherds in the story
of Jesus' birth. We usually think of their claim to fame as
being the first ones told of Jesus' birth. But perhaps these
lowly shepherds abiding in their fields were actually Jesus'
first disciples ... or pre-disciples, if you will! Consumed
with a desire to give Jesus honor, the shepherds actively
sought Jesus until they found him. They gave Jesus praise,
then proceeded to excitedly testify to others what they had
seen and heard. These were the actions and hearts of disciples—not just shepherds. What a powerful testimony and
example of discipleship we have in these lowly lords of the

hillsides! For if such seeking, loving, and witnessing attitudes were felt long before Jesus ever died for our sins, how much more should we seek to be his powerful, thankful disciples today!

What story is more beautiful, moving, and exciting to kids than the story of Jesus' birth? Yet kids often overlook another message in the Christmas story—how others honored Jesus and celebrated his arrival. Help kids learn that being a disciple is so exciting that we can celebrate Jesus' birth anytime of the year, just as the shepherds and angels celebrated on that silent night so long ago!

POWER FOCUS

Be sure you have the packages containing small nativity sets from last week.

As kids arrive, greet them with a smile and let them know you're glad they came. Then have kids sit in a circle and place the gift packages in the center of the circle. Review the Power Focus from last week. Say: **Last week I promised you special gifts, just as God had promised his people a special gift. What was the gift God promised his people?** Lead kids to tell the promise was for a Savior who would be a light to the Gentiles and the peace of the world. Then say: **We learned that disciples have faith in God's promises but sometimes have to wait for God to keep those promises. You had to wait for your promises, too!** Ask:

★ **How did it feel to wait for your special gift?**

★ **How is this like the way God's people probably felt as they waited for the promise of a Savior?**

Say: **God's promise was for everyone—and I have a gift for everyone!** Pass out the packages and let kids open their nativity sets. When the boxes are opened, ask:

★ **What was in your boxes?**

★ **How do these gifts remind us of God's special promise?**

Say: **Just think about that time long ago when the Israelites were waiting for God's promise to be kept! I can just imagine their excitement and anticipation. It was probably very hard to wait, don't you think? Today we'll learn about the night God kept his special promise, and** we'll discover that disciples seek, celebrate, and praise Jesus. You can help tell the joyous Bible story with your new nativity sets!

THE MIGHTY MESSAGE

Before class, arrange several large candles on tables near your story-telling area so the soft glow reaches around the room. If you choose not to use candles, use several flashlights or a small lamp to add a soft atmosphere to the darkened room as you tell the Christmas story. Play very soft instrumental Christmas music in the background. Be sure you include "Silent Night" as one of the songs.

Gather kids in your storytelling area and darken the room as you either light the candles or turn on the softer lights. Quietly say: **It was late at night, not too far from dawn. Cool dark surrounded the shepherds in their fields and their snoozing sheep. Place a shepherd figure in front of you and move it along with the story.** Pause. **Then all at once, an angel of the Lord appeared to the shepherds! Place an angel beside your shepherd.**

The shepherds were afraid! But the angel said, "Don't be afraid! We bring you great and joyous news! A Savior has been born in the city of David, and he has come for all people! You will find the baby wrapped in cloths and lying in a manger." Suddenly angels filled the sky and praised God saying, "Glory to God, and peace to men whom God loves!"

The shepherds were amazed and wanted to find this special baby in order to celebrate his birth and to honor him. So they went to Bethlehem, which was the city of David, and found Mary, Joseph, and baby Jesus, just as the angels had promised. They were in a stable with animals around them, and Jesus was lying in a manger all snuggly and warm! Place your gift box on its side to make a stable and set baby Jesus in his manger inside the stable. Set Mary and Joseph and a shepherd beside baby Jesus. Finally, place animals around the scene. Pause for kids to respond.

The shepherds honored and praised Jesus, then they ran to spread the news to others that the Savior of the world had been born! Have kids turn to one another and say, "Jesus is born! Thank you, God!"

POWER POINTERS

Create a life-size nativity scene by tracing kids' outlines on shelf paper. Color and cut them out. Tape them to a wall and glue straw to the manger. Add a cutout of baby Jesus before Christmas services!

Sing "Silent Night" with the Christmas tape or CD (or sing without music). Then turn on the lights and say: **You did a great job helping tell the Christmas story. Now you can answer questions with your nativity set. Hold up a shepherd figure if you know an answer.** Ask:

★ **How did the shepherds celebrate and praise Jesus?**

★ **In what ways did the shepherds demonstrate that they had the hearts of disciples?** (Lead kids to realize that the shepherds sought out Jesus, honored him, and told others about Jesus.)

★ **How did the angels celebrate Jesus' birth? How did they praise God?**

★ **How do you think Mary and Joseph celebrated Jesus' birth?**

Say: **God kept his promise to send a Savior into the world to love us and to forgive us of our sins. And when God sent his Son Jesus as our Savior, there was a celebration in many hearts! As disciples, we can celebrate Jesus, not just at Christmastime, but every day of our lives. Put your nativity sets away, and we'll learn more about how we can celebrate, honor, and praise Jesus as his loving disciples.**

THE MESSAGE IN **MOTION**

Be sure you have a party blow-out horn for each child and a selection of colorful markers. If you can find paper horns that are solid colored or that have generic celebratory designs, so much the better! Kids will be writing a message on the blow-out after unfurling it so that when the party horn is blown and the paper unfurls, they'll be able to read their messages. Be sure the disciple rap is taped to the wall or door. If you need to make a new copy, refer to page 18.

Gather kids and have them hold their Disciple Kit boxes and items. Say: **Last week we discovered that a disciple is one who learns from the master and that being a disciple of Jesus means we learn God's truths from him. We also started putting together a neat Disciple Kit last week and already have one item inside. Let's review from last week what a disciple knows. Hold your PVC pipe.** Lead kids in saying:

Truth 1: A disciple has faith in God's promises.

Say: **Good for you! Today we've learned a new truth about being a disciple: A disciple celebrates Jesus. And to remind us of this important truth, we'll be making party horns with a message.**

Disciples Celebrate Jesus!

Hand each child a party blow-out and have kids gently blow on the horns. As the paper unfurls, have kids place the horns on the table or floor and then write "Disciples celebrate Jesus!" on the length of the paper. When the messages are written, have kids gently roll the paper, then blow on the horns several times to roll and re-roll them. As kids work, play soft Christmas music in the background. When the horns are finished, ask:

★ **In what ways can we celebrate and honor Jesus?**

★ **Why do disciples want to get excited over Jesus and celebrate him as Savior?**

★ **How can we help others celebrate Jesus all year long?**

Say: **Isn't it wonderful that God sent Jesus to be our Savior?**

Listen to this super Scripture verse about why God sent us this most perfect gift. Read aloud John 3:16, then say: **God loved us so much he gave us Jesus! Wow! And we can be Jesus' loving disciples who seek, honor, and celebrate him. Let's chant our cool disciple rap from last week. When we're finished rapping, we'll end by blowing our party horns to celebrate Jesus—and to celebrate being his disciples!**

Have kids end by blowing their party horns, then flip the lights on and off for quiet. Say: **You now have two items in your Disciple Kits. Let's review both truths together. Hold up each item as we repeat the truth.**

Truth 1: A disciple has faith in God's promises. (PVC pipe)

Truth 2: A disciple celebrates Jesus. (party horn)

Say: **Great job! You're all learning to be wonderful disciples! Now remember, a disciple is someone who learns, and we can show that we're willing disciples by learning God's Word. Learning Scripture is a great way to honor and to celebrate Jesus as well! Jesus took the time to learn God's Word and we can, too.** Set aside the Disciple Kits until next week.

SUPER SCRIPTURE

Before class, make sure the newsprint with 1 John 4:14 written on it is still attached to the wall or a door. Make a new one if you need to. You'll also need to cut an 8-inch length of wide, colorful ribbon for each child.

Gather kids in front of the newsprint and repeat the verse in unison three times. Then ask kids who remembers the actions and pairs you put to the verse last week. Invite pairs of kids to stand and repeat the verse using the actions. Finish by repeating the verse and actions together.

We have seen and testify (Point to eyes and mouth.)
that the Father has sent his Son (Point upwards two times.)
to be the Savior of the world. (Make a finger cross, then arm circle.)
1 John 4:14

If you have older kids, introduce the extra challenge verse now.

Say: **Good for you! Learning God's Word can be fun and easy when we look for patterns just like the pairs we found in this verse! And this Mighty Memory Verse is such a good one to go along with celebrating the birth of Jesus. Think back to our Bible story and the shepherds who were first told of Jesus' birth. Think of what they did after the angels told them and then what they did after seeing baby Jesus.** Ask:

★ **How is this verse like what the shepherds might have said?**

★ **How did the shepherds see Jesus? How did they testify to others about him?**

★ **How is telling others about Jesus and what we've seen his love do a way to celebrate and honor Jesus?**

Say: **This is such an important verse, especially for us disciples! It reminds us that we can tell others about Jesus and how he was sent by God to be our Savior. What a good way to honor and praise Jesus! Let's make celebration ribbons using our Mighty Memory Verse to remind us to tell others about Jesus.**

Hand each child a length of ribbon and supply construction paper, markers, scissors, and tape. Have kids draw and cut out the pairs represented in 1 John 4:14 as follows:

★ eyes (for the word *seen*)
★ a smiling mouth (for the word *testify*)
★ a cloud with the word *Father*

★ a cloud with the word *Son*
★ a cross (for the word *Savior*)
★ a circle globe (for the word *world*)

Color the items and tape them down the length of the ribbons. Then say: **Let's use our celebration ribbons to repeat the Mighty Memory Verse, then we'll use our ribbons to share a prayer thanking God for his wonderful gift of Jesus!** Repeat the verse, pointing to each item on the ribbon. Then have kids form a circle.

A POWERFUL PROMISE

Before class, collect Christmas cards kids can write in. Ones with a nativity scene, angels, or bright stars will work best.

Have kids quietly hold their celebration ribbons, then ask for a moment of silence. Say: **We've been learning so much about being disciples. We've learned today that God kept his promise of a Savior and sent his Son Jesus to love us. We discovered that disciples celebrate, honor, and praise Jesus by telling others about him, seeking him, and learning God's Word. And we reviewed the Mighty Memory Verse that teaches us that God sent Jesus to us as our loving and forgiving Savior. First John 4:14 says** (pause and encourage kids to repeat the verse with you), **"We have seen and testify that the Father has sent his Son to be the Savior of the world."** (If you have older kids, repeat the extra challenge verse.)

Hold up the Bible and say: **It's wonderful to know that God keeps his promises and that he kept his promise to send us a Savior. God's promise of Jesus is something to celebrate, and we know that disciples celebrate Jesus every day! Let's make a promise to celebrate and praise Jesus every day during the next week. I'll hand each of you a Christmas card so you can write your promise on the card. Then you can tape the card to your door or a wall at home to remind you to celebrate, praise, and honor Jesus each day.** Help kids write the promises, which might say, "I will praise you, Jesus!" or "I celebrate Jesus!"

Have kids hold their celebration ribbons. Say: **We can use the Mighty Memory Verse to help us honor Jesus with a prayer. As we pray, point to each picture on your ribbon.**

Dear Lord, our *eyes* have seen and our *mouths* tell of the wonderful things you do for us each day! We're so glad our heavenly *Father* loves us and sent you, his *Son,* to love us, too. We celebrate that you are our powerful *Savior.* Please help us take your message of forgiveness and love throughout the *world.* In Jesus' name we pray, amen.

End with this responsive good-bye:

Leader: **May you always celebrate Jesus!**

Children: **And also you!**

Distribute the Power Page! take-home papers as kids are leaving and have kids take home their celebration ribbons and nativity sets. Thank children for coming and encourage them to keep their promises to Jesus this week.

POWER PAGE!

The Sweetest Story

Unscramble these words from the story of Jesus' birth. Use the clues from the Gospel of Luke to help you.

glaens _angels_ (2:15)

hesrdepsh _shepherds_ (2:8)

rvSioa _Savior_ (2:11)

melhtBehe _Bethlehem_ (2:4)

rgamne _manger_ (2:7)

eapce _peace_ (2:14)

CONFETTI CAKE

Make this yummy no-bake cake and sing "Happy Birthday" to Jesus with your family and friends to celebrate his glorious birth!

You'll need:

★ a pound cake   ★ whipped cream
★ a fork   ★ fruit-flavored gelatin
★ confetti candy sprinkles

Directions:

Mix the gelatin with hot water according to package directions. Poke holes in the pound cake with a fork. Pour liquid gelatin over the top of the cake, then chill several hours. Top with whipped cream and colorful candy sprinkles. Cut and serve.

Fill-'em-In — Maselina

Fit the words from 1 John 4:14 in the boxes. Cross off each word you use in the verse.

We have seen and testify that the father has sent his Son to be the Savior of the world.

1 John 4:14

LEARNING FOR THE LORD

Disciples learn about God.

Matthew 4:1-4
Luke 2:39-52

SESSION SUPPLIES

★ Bibles
★ shelf paper and a marker
★ a bolt of muslin
★ ½-inch wide elastic
★ small safety pins
★ scissors and fine-tipped markers
★ a picture of Jesus
★ tape and tacky craft glue
★ sliding matchboxes and construction paper
★ envelopes
★ colored tassels, rickrack, or other trim
★ photocopies of 1 John 4:14 (page 127)
★ photocopies of the Whiz Quiz (page 36) and the Power Page! (page 35)

MIGHTY MEMORY VERSE

We have seen and testify that the Father has sent his Son to be the Savior of the world. 1 John 4:14
(For older kids, add in John 1:14a: "The Word became flesh and made his dwelling among us.")

SESSION OBJECTIVES

During this session, children will
★ discover that Jesus learned about God
★ realize that disciples learn about God and Jesus
★ explore what Hebrew kids learned in Jesus' time
★ learn the importance of being teachable

BIBLE BACKGROUND

Of all the traits a disciple must possess, being teachable is perhaps the most important. Learning about God, his character, his truths, and his Word helps us make sound choices in serving, following, obeying, and worshiping him. Being teachable means earnestly seeking to learn—and that can mean hard work! Many people shy away from working to memorize Scripture, saying, "It's just too hard" or "I'm not good at it." Some would-be disciples plead "No time!" when it comes to faithfully reading the Bible every day in order to learn and remember what's read. But think! Even Jesus worked—yes, worked—to learn about God and to memorize Scripture. And it was this learning that helped empower Jesus to defeat Satan's temptations in Matthew 4. If Jesus felt the need to learn about his heavenly Father and took time to memorize his Word, we certainly have the same needs and can follow in his footsteps!

When it comes to school, perhaps the most often-asked question in a kids' repertoire is "*Why* do I have to learn that?" The same is true in Christian education. *Why* should we memorize God's Word? *Why* do we have to read the Bible? Kids need to realize that even Jesus spent precious hours learning about his Father and working to memorize his Word. Help kids understand that to be powerful disciples, we must do our homework!

POWER FOCUS

Before class, cut ½-inch wide elastic into 15-inch lengths and cut thin white muslin into 1-foot squares. Cut a fabric square and piece of elastic for each child. Before kids arrive, cover the door with a sheet of shelf paper that says "Welcome to Hebrew School. Shalom!" Draw scrolls around the door sign. Clear all chairs and tables from the room or push them to one side. Kids will sit on the floor today for their lesson, just as Hebrew kids would have done. You may wish to wear colorful clothing, including a bright cloak, tunic, or shawl and sandals.

Set out the elastic, fabric squares, small safety pins, and fine-tipped markers. As kids arrive, greet them warmly and say, "Shalom!" Encourage kids to repeat the greeting. Then say:

Shalom! I'm so glad to see each of you here at Hebrew school! You know, the best way to tell someone hello or good-bye in Hebrew is by the word *shalom,* which means "peace." Turn to three of your friends and greet them by saying, "Shalom."

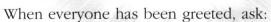

When everyone has been greeted, ask:

★ **Why do kids and some adults go to school?**

★ **How can learning help us in life? How can learning about God draw us closer to him? closer to Jesus?**

Say: **We all go to school, but did you know that kids back in the time Jesus lived also went to school? It was very different from our schools today, but they learned much of the same things: reading, writing, mathematics, and especially Scripture and God's truths. Hebrew school was usually for boys, but many girls were also able to attend.**

Today we'll be exploring what Jesus might have learned as a boy going to Hebrew school. We'll discover that disciples learn about God, just as Jesus did. We'll also learn about the time Jesus became the teacher to a group of adults! And we'll be learning new ways to praise the Lord and to say his name.

But first, you need to look more Hebrew-like. Each one of you needs to make a colorful headband or *kaffiyah* like Hebrew kids might have worn to school.

Hand each child a square of fabric and a piece of elastic. Let kids decorate the elastic and fabric with the markers, then pin the ends of the elastic together to make a headband. Have kids slide the headbands around their foreheads, then tuck the fabric squares under the elastic at the sides and backs of the headbands.

When the kaffiyahs are on, say: **Greet one more person by saying, "Shalom," then we'll discover how Jesus became the teacher when he was just a boy!**

POWER POINTERS

Play a simple Hebrew kids' game like Pick-Up Sticks. Collect twelve twigs all the same size. Take turns dropping and picking up twigs without disturbing the surrounding twigs. What cool fun!

THE MIGHTY MESSAGE

Before this activity, hide a picture of Jesus somewhere in your classroom or outside, if that's where your lesson is being held. Hide the picture so kids have to hunt but will eventually discover it.

Have kids sit around you on the floor or in the grass. Say: **Teachers in Jesus' day were usually called rabbis, and most were teachers in the temple and or in the synagogues where the Hebrews worshiped God. The word *rabbi* means master or teacher. When Jesus grew older, he was often referred to as rabbi, though Jesus knew there is only one master—God! The Bible tells us that, as Jesus grew from a very young child to a boy of about twelve, he grew in God's grace.** Read aloud Luke 2:40, then say: **When Jesus was twelve, his family and friends went to Jerusalem for the Passover Feast. There were many people present, and when Mary and Joseph left to return home, they thought Jesus was with relatives on the road ahead of them. But imagine their worry when they discovered Jesus was not there! What do you think they did?**

Allow kids to tell their ideas, then say: **Jesus' worried parents hurried back to Jerusalem. They looked everywhere for Jesus! I've hidden a picture of Jesus—see if you can find where Jesus is hiding!**

When the picture is found, continue the story: **They found Jesus in the temple teaching about God and answering the questions of the rabbis! Imagine—Jesus was doing the teaching, and he was only twelve years old! But Jesus had learned a great deal about God, and God had blessed him greatly.** Ask:

★ **Why was it so amazing for Jesus to be teaching about God?**

★ **Where and how do you think Jesus learned about his heavenly Father?**

★ **How did Jesus' learning about God show his love for the Father?**

★ **In what ways does our learning about God demonstrate our love for him?**

★ **Why is it important for disciples to learn all they can about God and Jesus?**

Say: **Jesus not only learned about God, he also took time to learn God's Word. That's a powerful example, isn't it? If Jesus wanted to learn about God and his Word, we can, too! A disciple learns about God and puts that learning into action.**

★ **How can learning about God help us live? help us get along with others?**

★ **How can learning about God and his Word help us steer clear of evil?**

Say: **There are many good reasons to learn about God, but one of the best is because that's what Jesus did! And strong disciples want to imitate Jesus. Let's make an unusual Hebrew item to add to our Disciple Kits to show we understand that disciples learn about God.**

THE MESSAGE IN MOTION

Set out the sliding matchboxes, construction paper, glue, scissors, markers, and tape. Explain to kids that long ago, in Jesus' time and before, Hebrew men made small boxes called phylacteries to wear on their foreheads and left arms. Tell kids that these boxes held portions of Scripture, including the Ten Commandments, and that people wore them to symbolize keeping God's Word close to their heads and hearts at all times.

Say: **Today we'll be making our own kind of phylacteries to remind us that disciples learn about God and his Word. We'll cover these tiny**

boxes with paper, then decorate them. Then we'll add an important message to the boxes, and later we'll add a Scripture verse.

Invite kids to work in pairs or trios and cut strips of construction paper to tape or glue around the outside of the matchboxes. Let kids use markers to decorate the boxes. Have kids cut 6-by-2-inch strips of paper and write "A disciple learns about God" on the strips.

Then fold the paper and slide it inside the phylacteries.

When the boxes are complete, say: **You now have three items in your Disciple Kit. Let's review all three disciple truths together. Hold up each item as we repeat the truth.**

Truth 1: A disciple has faith in God's promises. (PVC pipe)

Truth 2: A disciple celebrates Jesus. (party horn)

Truth 3: A disciple learns about God. (phylactery box)

Say: **Great job! Think of all that you're learning to help you be a powerful disciple! Hebrew kids heard stories about how God worked and helped people, and they made and wore the boxes to keep God's Word close. In Hebrew school, they also sang songs to honor the Lord. Let's repeat our disciple rap to show Jesus how glad we are to be his disciples *and* to be willing learners, just as he was!** See page 18 if you have forgotten the words to the rap.

Say: **Wow! I feel great being a disciple of Jesus, don't you? And it just keeps getting better the more we learn! Let's work on our Mighty Memory Verse just as the kids in Hebrew school worked to learn God's Word.**

SUPER SCRIPTURE

Before class, photocopy the Scripture strip for 1 John 4:14 from page 127 for each child. Cut each strip into five or six pieces and place them in an envelope for each child.

Gather kids and repeat 1 John 4:14 in unison three times. Then invite pairs of kids to repeat the verse using the actions they learned the last two weeks. Finish by repeating the verse and actions together. (If you have older kids, repeat the extra challenge verse in pairs, too.)

We have seen and testify (Point to eyes and mouth.)
that the Father has sent his Son (Point upwards two times.)
to be the Savior of the world. (Make a finger cross, then arm circle.)
1 John 4:14

Say: **You're remembering this verse so well! You know, back in Jesus' time there weren't a lot of books as we know them, and they didn't have lots of neat pens, markers, and paper to write the verses. They had to learn God's Word by repeating and memorizing it. Even Jesus memorized God's Word, and he used it to fight Satan.** Read aloud Matthew 4:1-4, then ask:

★ **How does learning God's Word draw us closer to God? make us better disciples?**

★ **What can we learn from 1 John 4:14 about Jesus? How can this verse help us be stronger disciples?**

Say: **Knowing this verse helps us understand that Jesus is God's Son and that God sent him as a Savior for the world—and that we can tell others this wonderful news! It's hard work learning God's Word, but there's no work that's more worth it!**

Learning God's Word is also fun! I have Mighty Memory Verse puzzles for you to assemble. When you've taped the puzzle together correctly, read the verse to a friend, then place the verse in your phylactery.

Allow several minutes for kids to assemble their puzzles and place them in the Disciple Kits. Then say: **There's one more important thing kids in Hebrew school did every day. Let's form a circle, and we'll discover what that was.**

A POWERFUL PROMISE

Before class, cut a 2-by-1-foot piece of muslin for each child. You'll also need to cut tassels, rickrack, or other trim to go along the short ends of the fabric. Kids will be making prayer shawls, so they'll need tacky craft glue and markers as well.

Hand each child a marker, two lengths of trim, and a piece of fabric. Say: **In Hebrew school, kids prayed to thank God for his love, his forgiveness, his saving grace, and his provision. Often people who prayed would wear prayer shawls into the temple. We'll make prayer shawls as we remember all we learned today. First, we learned how to greet others in Hebrew. Write the word** *shalom* **on your prayer shawl to show how we can greet one another and God.** Pause for kids to write.

Next we learned that disciples learn about God. Draw a heart to show that, because we love the Lord, we want to learn about him.

Allow kids to draw hearts, then continue: **We also learned about the time Jesus went to the temple to teach others about God. Draw a cross to remind us that Jesus showed us how to be teachable and to learn about God and his Word.**

Finally, we discovered that learning God's Word helps from one end of our lives to another. Glue the trim to both short ends of your prayer shawls. Don't use too much glue because we'll be wearing our shawls in a moment!

After the shawls are finished, have kids drape them over one shoulder, then form a circle and hold hands. Say: **Let's pray. Dear Lord, we thank you that Jesus was wise and taught others and us with such love and authority. We're glad Jesus set an example for us by learning about you and your Word. Please help us always remain teachable and ready to learn and then put that learning to use in our lives. Amen.**

Let's end by promising God to remain teachable and willing to learn. Silently say, "Lord, I will learn about you my whole life." Then write your name on your prayer shawl to remind you of your important promise.

Before kids leave, allow five or ten minutes to complete the Whiz Quiz from page 36. If you run out of time, be sure to do this page first thing next week. The Whiz Quiz is an invaluable tool that allows kids, teachers, and parents see what kids have learned in the previous three weeks.

End with this responsive good-bye:

Leader: **May you always be a teachable disciple.**

Children: **And also you!**

Distribute the Power Page! take-home papers as kids are leaving and remind them to take home their kaffiyahs and prayer shawls. Thank children for coming and encourage them to keep their promises this week.

POWER PAGE!

Hebrew School

In Jesus' time, boys and many girls went to school to learn reading, writing, and to do Bible studies. Use the Hebrew letters to discover what nickname God's "studying" people earned.

The people of the book

B E F H K
L O P T

Divine Lessons

Disciples love to learn about God. Read from the Psalms to learn more about who God is and what he does.

God is _____ and _____ . (24:8)

God is our _____ . (23:1)

God's ways are _____ . (77:13)

God's kingdom is _____ . (145:13)

God is _____ and loves _____ .
(99:4)

God made the _____ and _____ .
(95:5)

God's commands are _____ . (19:8)

SCRAMBLER

Unscramble the words to 1 John 4:14. Write the correct words on the spaces under each mixed-up word.

eW	ahve	esne	nda	tefisty	hatt	het	aFthre	sha
We	have	seen	and	testify			Father	has

nest	shi	Sno	ot	eb	eth	Sorvia	fo	het	rowld
			to	be			of		

WHIZ QUIZ

Color in YES or NO to answer each question.

✳ A disciple is a follower who learns.   (YES) (NO)

✳ God promised us a Savior.   (YES) (NO)

✳ Disciples don't need to learn God's Word.   (YES) (NO)

✳ Jesus taught in the temple as a young boy.   (YES) (NO)

✳ Jesus didn't have to learn about God.   (YES) (NO)

✳ It's important to keep learning about God.   (YES) (NO)

✳ God only keeps some of his promises.   (YES) (NO)

✳ Disciples praise and honor Jesus.   (YES) (NO)

AIM THE ARROWS

Draw arrows to place the words in their correct positions to complete the Mighty Memory Verse. The first word has been done for you.

testify   We   that   seen   the   and

have

We ___ ___ ___ ___ ___ ___

his

___ ___ ___ ___ ___

sent

___ ___ ___ ___ ___ ___

the

___ ___ ___ ___ ___ .   1 ___ 4:14

father

has

the

be

to

world   John   Son   Savior   of

JESUS' MIRACLES

That at the name of Jesus
every knee should bow, in heaven
and on earth and under the
earth, and every tongue confess
that Jesus Christ is Lord, to the
glory of God the Father.
Philippians 2:10, 11

Lesson 4

Disciples trust Jesus to help.

Matthew 8:23-27
Romans 15:13
John 14:1

SESSION SUPPLIES

★ Bibles
★ a bouncy ball
★ small baby-food jars with lids
★ tacky craft glue
★ glitter and sparkly confetti pieces
★ corn syrup and plastic spoons
★ 2-inch plastic boats (party favors)
★ florists' clay
★ newsprint and markers
★ cranberry and apple juice concentrate
★ ginger ale and licorice sticks
★ self-sealing plastic bags and ice cubes
★ photocopies of the Power Page! (page 45)

SEA OF TRUST

MIGHTY MEMORY VERSE

That at the name of Jesus every knee should bow, in heaven and on earth and under the earth, and every tongue confess that Jesus Christ is Lord. Philippians 2:10, 11

SESSION OBJECTIVES

During this session, children will
★ discover that Jesus is in control of everything
★ realize that disciples trust Jesus in all things
★ learn that trusting Jesus demonstrates love
★ thank Jesus that we can trust him

BIBLE BACKGROUND

Trust is a word we tend to use so often in surface ways that we tend to forget the depth of its meaning. Synonyms for *trust* include *confidence, certainty, assurance,* and *faith.* These powerful words read like the character description of the only one worthy of our complete trust: Jesus! Perhaps that's why Jesus rebuked his disciples for their lack of confidence as they rode the stormy sea long ago. The tumultuous sea threatened their lives and created fear as turbulent as the pounding waves. In the midst of this, the disciples forgot one important fact that should have assuaged their fears and given them the certainty of a safe landing: *Jesus was with them!* When we truly place all our faith in Jesus, we begin to understand what it means to approach life with radical assurance of our Savior's loving help. It means ... *trust!*

Kids often find it easy to place their trust in anyone and anything—after all, who would want to be mean to a kid? But they also need to recognize that false trust and security lie in things such as money, earthly heroes, and hollow words. Use this lesson to equip kids to recognize that the one true place to put our trust is in the saving grace and power of our Lord Jesus!

POWER FOCUS

Clear a playing area in the center of the room or go to a place where kids can spread out, such as a yard, playground, or fellowship hall.

Greet kids warmly as they arrive and have them form two teams and stand on opposite sides of the room. Tell kids to find partners on their teams and explain that you're going to begin with a lively game of partner dodge ball. Say: **In this exciting game, you have an important job. You must guard your partner from being tagged by the ball. Decide in your pairs right now who will be the first guard and take guard duty!** Pause for kids to decide. **Guards can deflect the ball with arms or legs, but the partners being guarded cannot touch the ball at all. If a partner is tagged, he or she becomes the guard. If both partners are tagged, they must sit out on the sidelines. Whenever you hear me call "switch," switch places so the guards become the guarded and vice versa! One more rule: please keep the ball at knee level or below when trying to tag someone!**

Begin the game by tossing the ball to a team. Continue playing for five minutes or until only one pair is left, then call time. Be sure to call out "switch" several times during the game. End the game with kids giving each other rousing high fives.

When the game is over, have kids take a breather and ask:

★ **How did trust play a part in this game?**

★ **Did you trust your partner to help? Why or why not?**

★ **How is this game like relying on Jesus' help?**

★ **In what areas of our lives do we rely on Jesus' help?**

Say: **Sometimes we need a helping hand, and it's important to be able to trust the one helping us. We rely on Jesus for so many things, including safety, helping in prayer, teaching us to obey God, and staying near us. If we didn't trust Jesus, we couldn't rely on him or feel secure in his** care! Disciples especially must learn to trust Jesus, and that's what we'll be learning about today.

We'll discover how Jesus' first disciples learned to trust him with their very lives one dark, stormy night. We'll add another fun item to our Disciple Kits, and we'll also learn a new Mighty Memory Verse that helps us trust Jesus' power to help! Now let's sit in a circle on the floor and get ready to hear about a stormy night long ago. We'll even use our ball to help tell the Bible story!

THE MIGHTY MESSAGE

Say: **This is such an exciting story. Let's pretend that our circle is the sea and this ball is a boat on the sea. We'll begin by rolling the ball slowly to show that the little boat was sailing along and having a lovely time in the water.** Begin rolling the ball back and forth around the circle and continue as you retell the story of Jesus calming the sea from Matthew 8:23-27.

POWER POINTERS

Help children remember the meaning of real trust in Jesus with this memorable acronym:
True
Reliance
Under
Sticky
Times!

It was late at night, and Jesus had been teaching others to obey God. Jesus and his disciples climbed into a wooden boat and started out across the Sea of Galilee. The stars were out, the sea was calm, and the night was beautiful. Jesus, tired from his long day, lay down to rest and soon fell asleep.

While Jesus was sleeping, big storm clouds filled the sky, and a crashing storm came upon the sea! The wind blew, and the waves tossed the boat about on the sea! Roll the ball faster around the circle. **The disciples looked at one another and were very afraid. "We'll drown!" they said. So they ran to wake Jesus. Jesus stood in the bow of the boat and asked his disciples, "Why do you have so little faith?" Then Jesus turned to face the wind and waves, and he spoke with authority. "Be still!" he said. The wind stopped blowing, and the waves stopped flowing!** Stop and hold the ball.

The disciples looked at one another again. Who is this that even the wind and the waves obey him, they wondered. But the disciples had learned an important lesson, that we can trust Jesus with our lives when we know, love, and follow him!

Say: **That was a great Bible story, and Jesus really did help his disciples in an amazing way. Let's see how much you learned from this story. I'll ask a question and bounce the ball to someone in the circle to answer. If you think you need help, simply roll the ball to someone else!** Ask these questions and roll the ball to a different child each time.

★ **Why was it wise for the disciples to ask Jesus to help them?**

★ **Why do you think Jesus said the disciples had no faith?**

★ **In what ways does trusting Jesus help us in times of trouble or worries?**

★ **How does it help us to know that Jesus is in control of everything?**

★ **What can we learn about trusting Jesus from this Bible story?**

Hold the ball and say: **Jesus is so powerful that he is in control of everything. And we can trust his power to help us at all times. Let's stand in the circle, and I'll bounce the ball to someone. That person can tell one thing to trust Jesus with, such as "I trust Jesus with my prayers" or "I trust Jesus to help me."**

Continue naming times and ways to trust Jesus, then say: **The first disciples trusted Jesus when a storm in their life seemed out of control. Let's make cool boats-in-a-bottle to remind us that we can trust Jesus when our own troubles and worries seem out of control!**

THE MESSAGE IN **MOTION**

Before class, collect tiny boats from a party supply store or department store. If you can't find tiny plastic boats, let kids model their own from florists' clay.

Set out the baby-food jars and lids, florists' clay, glue, glitter, confetti, spoons, and corn syrup. Hand each child a small boat or a clump of clay to model a boat. Show kids how use clay to attach the boats to the insides of the lids, as in the illustration.

Then help kids fill the jars two-thirds full of corn syrup. Sprinkle in a teaspoon of confetti and glitter as "rain," then place glue around the inside of the lid. Screw the lids in place securely and set the jars upside down in the Disciple Kits to dry.

Say: **As our lids dry, we'll continue learning more about being disciples. You now have four things in your Disciple Kit, so let's review all four disciple truths together. Hold up each item as we repeat the truth.**

Truth 1: A disciple has faith in God's promises. (PVC pipe)

Truth 2: A disciple celebrates Jesus. (party horn)

Truth 3: A disciple learns about God. (phylactery box)

Truth 4: A disciple trusts Jesus. (boat-in-a-bottle)

Say: **Good for you! It's fun learning to be disciples, isn't it? And what a great teacher we have in Jesus! I know Jesus' first disciples were proud and excited to be disciples, and that's the same way I feel knowing I'm a disciple for Jesus. Jesus is in control of everything, and that makes trusting him feel so good. In fact, I feel good enough to rap out a rhythm, how about you? Let's repeat our disciple rap and clap along with the words!**

Lead kids in repeating the disciple rap you've been learning for the last couple of weeks. Add the new verse and repeat the rhyme once more.

I'm not just a follower—that couldn't be much hollower!
I'm not just a sin-quitter, quiet Christian, pew-sitter!
I'M A DISCIPLE! A DISCIPLE OF JESUS!

I learn the lessons Jesus taught;
I know my life by him was bought;
Jesus is my every thought—
I'M A DISCIPLE! A DISCIPLE OF JESUS!

I trust in help that Jesus brings;
He's in control of everything;
I'll praise his name and shout and sing—
I'M A DISCIPLE! A DISCIPLE OF JESUS!

Say: **I'm so glad we're disciples! And as disciples, we have the responsibility to learn all we can about Jesus, God, and God's Word. So let's begin learning a new Mighty Memory Verse that tells why we can trust Jesus.**

SUPER SCRIPTURE

Purchase large cans of juice concentrate, but don't mix the juice with water. You'll need a large can of cranberry and one of apple for every ten kids. You'll also need a two-liter bottle of ginger ale and lots of ice cubes and chewy licorice sticks.

Gather kids, have them open their Bibles to Philippians 2:10, 11, and read the following: **"That at the name of Jesus every knee should bow, in** heaven and on earth and under the earth, and every tongue confess that Jesus Christ is Lord." (Kids will learn the rest of verse 11 next week.) Then say: **What a powerful verse telling us of Jesus' authority! Just think, at the name of Jesus, everyone on, above, and under the earth will do two things: go down on bended knee and admit that Jesus is Lord! Let's do that right now. When I say Jesus' name, you kneel and say, "Jesus Christ is Lord!" If I say any other name, stand still and remain quiet.**

Alternate saying Jesus' name and naming other names. After several calls, invite a child to call out either Jesus' name or some other name. When you're through playing, repeat the Mighty Memory Verse two more times, then say: **This Mighty Memory Verse tells us that Jesus is so powerful that everyone will know that he is Lord. It's wonderful to be Jesus' disciples who can confess and tell others that he is our all-powerful Lord whom we trust with our lives! Let's celebrate our trust with a treat, but you have to trust me that it will taste good and trust yourselves to follow directions in preparing it!**

Open the concentrated juices and the ginger ale. Hand each child a self-sealing plastic sandwich bag and say: **First we'll place three ice cubes in our bags, then add one spoon full of each juice and squish them gently together.** Pause while kids add the ice and frozen juice to their bags. **Now we'll fill our bags half full of ginger ale, then pop in a licorice straw for sweet sipping!** Have kids seal their bags after they add the ginger ale, then open one end to slip in the licorice straws.

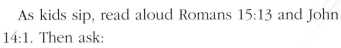

As kids sip, read aloud Romans 15:13 and John 14:1. Then ask:

★ **How does it help to obey Jesus, just as we obeyed the directions for our treats?**

★ **In what ways does trusting Jesus demonstrate our love for him?**

★ **Why are you glad you're a disciple who trusts and obeys Jesus?**

Say: **Mmm, these treats are great, and so is trusting Jesus! Let's end by offering a prayer thanking Jesus for his power, love, and trustworthiness.** Toss the plastic bags in the trash.

A POWERFUL PROMISE

Before class, write the words to the marching song in this activity on newsprint and tape the newsprint to a wall or door for kids to read. Keep the words for the next few weeks until kids know the words.

Have kids sit in a circle and ask for a moment of silence, then say: **We've learned today that Jesus is in control of everything, even the wind and waves. We've discovered that disciples trust Jesus with their lives. And we've started to learn a new Mighty Memory Verse that teaches us that everyone will know Jesus' power. Philippians 2:10, 11 says** (pause and encourage kids to repeat the verse with you), **"That at the name of Jesus every knee should bow, in heaven and on earth and under the earth, and every tongue confess that Jesus Christ is Lord."**

Hold the Bible and say: **As disciples, we know we can trust Jesus to help us because Jesus is in control of everything. Just as Jesus wanted his first disciples to trust him on the stormy sea that night long ago, Jesus wants his disciples today to trust him. Let's promise to trust Jesus even more this week. Let's pass the Bible around our circle and say, "I will put my trust in you, Jesus."** Pass the Bible until everyone has had a chance to make a promise.

Then say: **Let's end by learning a new marching song about being a powerful disciple of Jesus. Here are the words** (point to the newsprint), **and they go like this!** As kids read the words, sing them to the tune of the old camp favorite, "The Ants Go Marching One-By-One." Clap on the Xs.

Oh, I'm a disciple of the Lord, hurrah! (XX), *hurrah!* (XX)
Oh, I'm a disciple of the Lord, hurrah! (XX), *hurrah!* (XX)
J-E-S-U-S is his name.
His power and glory I'll always proclaim.
I'm a d-i-s-c-i (XX) *p-l-e* (XX) *that's all I* (XX) *want to be!*
Boom, boom, boom, boom! Boom, boom, boom ... (repeat the song)

End with this responsive good-bye:
Leader: **May you always trust Jesus.**
Children: **And also you!**
Distribute the Power Page! take-home papers as kids are leaving. Thank kids for coming and encourage them to keep their promises this week.

POWER PAGE!

WHATTA STORY!

Number the events in their correct order to retell how Jesus calmed the storm from Matthew 8:23-27. Then illustrate your favorite story scene.

❑ A mighty storm came upon the sea.

❑ The disciples were amazed!

❑ Jesus was sleeping in the boat.

❑ Jesus calmed the wind and waves.

❑ The disciples woke Jesus.

Stormy Sea Sippers

Sip this sparkling delight as you read Matthew 8:23-27 and praise Jesus for his power and loving care!

You'll need:
★ a clear bottle or glass
★ sparkling apple juice
★ blue food coloring
★ a straw
★ a large peanut "boat"

Directions:
Mix the sparkling apple juice and a few drops of blue food coloring in a clear bottle or glass. Drop in your peanut boat and watch it float! Sip away but save the boat for last!

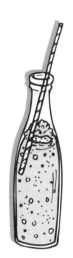

Use the word bank to complete Philippians 2:10, 11a.

That at _____ _____ of

_____ every _____ should

bow, in _____ and on

_____ and _____ the

earth, and _____ _____

_____ that Jesus _____ is

_____ .   Philippians 2:10, 11a

Word Bank Wonder

Jesus	under
heaven	every
Christ	confess
knee	tongue
Lord	name
the	earth

45

HELPED AND HEALED!

Disciples seek Jesus.

Luke 5:17-26
Matthew 7:7, 8

SESSION SUPPLIES

★ Bibles
★ scissors and markers
★ copy paper
★ sunglasses (see The Message in Motion)
★ paint pens and glitter glue
★ tacky craft glue and tape
★ plastic jewels, sequins, and feathers
★ photocopies of Philippians 2:10, 11 (page 127)
★ photocopies of the Power Page! (page 53)

MIGHTY MEMORY VERSE

That at the name of Jesus every knee should bow, in heaven and on earth and under the earth, and every tongue confess that Jesus Christ is Lord, to the glory of God the Father. Philippians 2:10, 11

(For older kids, add in Romans 6:23: "For the wages of sin is death, but the gift of God is eternal life in Christ Jesus our Lord.")

SESSION OBJECTIVES

During this session, children will
★ realize that Jesus can do anything
★ understand that disciples seek Jesus
★ discover that disciples serve others
★ praise Jesus for his power in our lives

BIBLE BACKGROUND

What's the toughest thing you've had to search for in the past week? Your car keys, a bit of free time, peace of mind, or perhaps your favorite recipe for the church potluck? All too often we get so caught up seeking things of small substance that we overlook the one we should be seeking, the one who will help us find everything we need—Jesus! When we seek Jesus and his teaching with all our hearts and spirits, we discover a peace that truly passes all understanding, a serenity and singleness of purpose that is as divine as it is useful to our lives.

Kids adore Hide-and-Seek and are willing to play the game almost any-time. Although seeking Jesus in our lives is not a game, kids will recognize the power of finding answers, help, and security as they seek the Lord with all their hearts. Use this lesson to help kids understand that disciples seek Jesus all their lives and find him in nearly every place they look.

POWER FOCUS

Before class, practice this cool paper-cutting trick so your presentation will be smooth during class. To help kids actually step through a piece of copy paper, simply cut the paper in four strips lengthwise, then tape the strips end to end to make one long strip of paper. Give the strip a twist and tape the two ends, front and back. Then poke scissors through the center of the strip and cut all the way around the loop to where you started. When you hold the paper up, you'll see an amazing circle large enough to easily step through! Kids will be cutting their own loops, so have plenty of paper, tape, and scissors.

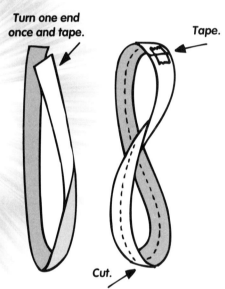

Turn one end once and tape.

Tape.

Cut.

Warmly greet each child and have kids find partners. Ask a pair of kids to come forward and hand each child a sheet of paper. Say: **I'd like to ask you to step through this paper if you're able.** Pause for kids' reactions, then say: **It does seem impossible, doesn't it? But I'm here to help you accomplish this goal! In fact, let's give everyone a sheet of paper, and I'll help all of you do this seemingly impossible feat.**

Hand each person a piece of paper and supply plenty of scissors and tape. Have kids follow along as you cut the strips, create a long strip, form the loop, and tape the ends of the strip. Show kids how to poke their scissors through the paper and cut clear around the loop.

When the cutting is complete, say: **Now stand up and see if you can step through your papers!** When kids have all stepped through their amazing loops, give a lively round of applause and ask them to be seated again. Ask:

★ **Did you think this trick could be done so easily? Explain.**

★ **How was my help useful? In what ways did I help others?**

★ **How is this like the way Jesus helps us do seemingly impossible things when we seek him?**

★ **How can we let Jesus know that we need him and seek his help?** Say: **Jesus devoted his entire life to helping and serving others, often in amazing ways! But the people of his day discovered that they needed to ask Jesus for his help and guidance in their lives. As Jesus' disciples, we can seek Jesus and his help, too! Today we'll be discovering why seeking Jesus is an important part of discipleship. We'll learn about a time Jesus helped a man in an amazing way and why that man showed good discipleship qualities. And we'll keep working on our Mighty Memory Verse that tells us about Jesus' authority and how everyone will know that Jesus is Lord. Right now, let's use our paper loops to tell the story of how Jesus helped and healed a man long ago.**

THE **MIGHTY** MESSAGE

POWER POINTERS

Play a quick game of Hide-and-Seek. Take turns hiding a sticker of Jesus or a paper cross and letting kids seek to find it. Once the item is found say, "I've found Jesus!"

Have kids spread out around the room and say: **Our story, which comes from the book of Luke, is about a time Jesus was teaching and healing people in a crowded house. I'll tell the story and have you do things with your paper loops to help. Listen carefully.**

Long ago there was a man who couldn't walk. All day and night he lay on a mat wishing and hoping that someday he could walk, hop, jump, and run. Have kids spread their loops on the floor and lay inside them like mats. Continue: **But this man had good friends who were excited because they had heard Jesus was nearby healing people. Maybe Jesus could help the crippled man, too! So the friends carried the man and went to find Jesus.** Have kids stand and hold their loops as they walk around the room one time.

Then say: **When they found the house Jesus was teaching and healing in, they tried to go through the door.** Instruct kids to walk forward through the loops. **But the crowd was too big, and they couldn't get through any doors!** Have kids walk backward through their loops. **Maybe they could go through the window, they thought.** Have kids crawl forward through their loops. **But alas! The rooms were too crowded to go through the windows either!** Tell children to crawl backwards through their paper loops. **Oh! They wanted so much to get to Jesus! Why,** they'd do almost anything to find him! Then the friends had a wonderful idea! They'd climb the steps to the rooftop and try from there. So up they went. Have kids hold their loops and take pretend steps upward.

The roof was made of tiles, and there was a hole through some of the tiles right above where Jesus was teaching! So the men lowered their friend down, down, down through the hole in the roof! Have kids lower the paper loops downward over their heads to the floor, then lay on the loops as mats. The crippled man was right in front of Jesus. He had found Jesus at last. Yeah! Lead kids in a round of applause. Then Jesus said, "Friend, your sins are forgiven. Get up and walk!" Have kids stand up and walk, then hop and jump for joy. And the man stood and took his mat and went home praising God! Lead kids in a march around the room praising God by saying, "God helped me walk! He's the best!" After kids have walked around the room once, have them sit inside their paper loops and ask:

★ Why did the man and his friends seek Jesus?

★ In what ways is this like how we should seek Jesus all the time, not just when we have problems?

★ How can we seek Jesus in our own lives?

Say: Jesus wants us to seek him all the time. When we have troubles and need help, we can seek Jesus. When we're feeling great and want to thank Jesus for all he does, we can seek him. When we just need someone to talk to, we can seek Jesus. In Matthew 7 Jesus talks about seeking and finding. Read aloud Matthew 7:7, 8. Then ask:

★ What good things come from seeking Jesus and finding him?

★ How can you help someone else seek Jesus?

Say: We've been learning about being disciples these past few weeks, and it's important to know that a disciple seeks Jesus all the time. Let's add another neat item to our Disciple Kits to remind us that looking for Jesus always keeps our focus on him!

THE MESSAGE IN MOTION

Before class, either purchase a pair of inexpensive plastic sunglasses or enlarge and photocopy the sunglasses pattern from page 124 on stiff neon paper, one for each child.

Set out craft items to decorate the glasses, including markers, paint pens, glitter glue, tacky craft glue, plastic jewels, sequins, and feathers.

Gather kids around the craft table and hand each child a pair of plastic or paper sunglasses to decorate. Explain that these glasses will represent seeking or looking for Jesus and will be fun reminders that disciples seek Jesus all the time. As kids work to decorate their nifty eye wear, ask questions such as, "Why do we need to have Jesus as our main focus in life" and "What might happen if we stop seeking the Lord?"

When the glasses are complete, have kids model their shades and rap to the disciple rap from page 42.

Say: **And as disciples, we always seek Jesus! You look so neat in your super shades. But let's put them in our Disciple Kits so we can review the truths of being a disciple with the other items, too. Hold up each item as we repeat that particular truth.**

Truth 1: A disciple has faith in God's promises. (PVC pipe)

Truth 2: A disciple celebrates Jesus. (party horn)

Truth 3: A disciple learns about God. (phylactery box)

Truth 4: A disciple trusts Jesus. (boat-in-a-bottle)

Truth 5: A disciple seeks Jesus. (sunglasses)

Say: **Great job! You know, remembering these important disciple truths can help us become powerful disciples of Jesus, and that's awesome! Something else that can help us become even stronger disciples of Jesus is learning God's Word. Let's turn our attention to the Mighty Memory Verse as we continue to learn about Jesus and how we can be his dynamite disciples!**

SUPER SCRIPTURE

Before this activity, make sure you've photocopied the Scripture strip for Philippians 2:10, 11 from page 127 for each child. You'll also need to write this verse on paper and tape it to a wall or door for kids to read.

Repeat the Mighty Memory Verse two times in unison: **"That at the name of Jesus every knee should bow, in heaven and on earth and under the earth, and every tongue confess that Jesus Christ is Lord."** Then say:

**Let's add one more short part to this verse since you're doing so
well learning it! The last part says, "to the glory of God the Father."**
Have kids repeat that portion of the verse two times, then repeat the entire
verse with the new portion added two more times. If you have older kids
and want an extra Scripture challenge, introduce the extra challenge verse
at this time.

Then have kids look at the verse on the wall or door and use portions of the verse to answer these questions:

★ **At the name of Jesus, what will happen first?** (Every knee will
   bow.)

★ **Where will this happen?** (in heaven, on the earth, and under the earth)

★ **At the name of Jesus, what will happen next?** (Every tongue will confess that Jesus Christ is Lord.)

★ **Why will every tongue confess that Jesus Christ is Lord?** (to the
   glory of God the Father)

Say: **This important verse tells us what will happen when the name of
Jesus Christ is spoken and why that will happen. This verse tells us of
Jesus' power and authority in heaven, on the earth, and under the
earth. Let's use our paper loops to play a game that will help us remember this long but very important verse.**

Spread the loops around the room in a large circle and have kids stand in
their loops. Number kids alternately as ones and twos around the circle. Have
the ones respond to "every knee should bow" and kneel down. As they kneel,
have them say, "in heaven and on earth and under the earth." Then have the
twos respond to "every tongue confess" by jumping up and saying, "Jesus
Christ is Lord, to the glory of God the Father."

Continue two times, then switch groups and responses. End the game by having kids tape the Scripture strips for Philippians 2:10, 11 to their paper loops.

When you're finished, have kids sit inside their paper loops. Say: **Disciples
recognize that Jesus is Lord and that he is all-powerful in heaven, on
earth, and under the earth. And disciples know it's important to seek
Jesus and his power at all times. Let's share a prayer thanking Jesus for
his loving help when we seek him with all our hearts.**

A POWERFUL PROMISE

Be sure the words to the new disciple marching song kids learned last week
are on the wall. If you need to make a new copy, see page 44.

Ask for a moment of silence, then say: **Close your eyes for a moment. Where do you find Jesus? Can you find him in your thoughts?** Pause. **Can you see him in your heart?** Pause. **Are you able to feel Jesus' love within your spirit?** Pause, then say: **We can find Jesus in so many places and in so many people: in kind words and encouraging thoughts, in answered prayers and loving hugs. Disciples seek Jesus all the time to help, heal, give, forgive, and guide them through their lives. Philippians 2:10, 11 tells us of Jesus' power and authority. Repeat the verse with me.** Lead kids in saying, **"That at the name of Jesus every knee should bow, in heaven and on earth and under the earth, and every tongue confess that Jesus Christ is Lord, to the glory of God the Father."** If you have older kids, repeat the extra challenge verse, too.

Continue: **Let's offer a prayer thanking Jesus for always being close by when we look for him, for always helping when we ask, and for always being available when we seek him.** Pause, then pray: **Dear Jesus, we're so thankful that you love us enough to be there when we need you and seek you out. Because we love you and want to keep our focus on you, we will seek you all our lives. Please help us look for you in all we say and do. In your precious name we pray, amen.**

Say: **Jesus promises to be there every time we seek him, just as he was there for the crippled man. Sometimes we must seek very diligently to find Jesus, but he's always waiting for us and ready to help us. Let's make a promise to Jesus, too. We can promise to seek him in all we do this week. Let's go around the circle and tap one another on the shoulder. When you're tapped, say, "Jesus, I will seek you because I love you."** Continue around the circle until everyone has made a promise.

End by singing the new disciple song you learned last week to the tune of "The Ants Go Marching One-By-One." Clap on the Xs as you march around the room.

End with this responsive good-bye:

Leader: **May you seek Jesus in all you do.**

Children: **And also you!**

Distribute the Power Page! take-home papers as kids are leaving and remind kids to take home their paper loops. Thank children for coming and encourage them to keep their promises this week.

POWER PAGE!

HELPED-N-HEALED

Jesus served others in many ways, one of which was by healing them. Match the verses with who was healed.

Matthew 9:6-8   cured a man of leprosy

Mark 1:30, 31   healed a crippled man

Luke 7:6-10   cured a servant

Matthew 8:2, 3   cured woman of fever

WORD FUN!

Read the clues and fill in the words. When you read the circled letters downward, you'll discover something that all disciples do!

1. not frown   ◯ _ _ _ _

2. food from hens   ◯ _ _ _

3. color of some apples   ◯ _ _

4. musical instrument

◯ _ _ _ _

5. come in!   ◯ _ _ _ _

Try This! LETTER BEFORE

Write the letter that comes <u>before</u> the letter under each space to complete Philippians 2:10, 11.

that at the name of _ _ _ _ _ _ every _ _ _ _ should _ _ _ ,
U I B U   O B N F   K F T V T   L O F F   C P X

in _ _ _ _ _ _ and on _ _ _ _ _ and _ _ _ _ _ the earth, and
I F B W F O   F B S U I   V O E F S

_ _ _ _ _ _ _ _ _ _ _ _ _ _ confess that Jesus _ _ _ _ _ _ is _ _ _ _
F W F S Z U P O H V F   D I S J T U   M P S E

to the _ _ _ _ _ of God the Father.
H M P S Z

SERVING MIRACLES!

Disciples serve Jesus and others.

Mark 1:29-31
Luke 5:4-11; 17:11-19
Galatians 5:13

SESSION SUPPLIES

★ Bibles
★ plastic spoons
★ foam packing peanuts
★ pencils and tacky craft glue
★ opaque paint pens
★ fine-tipped permanent markers
★ felt and fabric scraps
★ thick yarn or fake craft hair
★ photocopies of the Why, What, How? handout (page 124)
★ photocopies of the Whiz Quiz (page 62) and the Power Page! (page 61)

MIGHTY MEMORY VERSE

That at the name of Jesus every knee should bow, in heaven and on earth and under the earth, and every tongue confess that Jesus Christ is Lord, to the glory of God the Father. Philippians 2:10, 11

(For older kids, add in Romans 6:23: "For the wages of sin is death, but the gift of God is eternal life in Christ Jesus our Lord.")

SESSION OBJECTIVES

During this session, children will
★ realize that Jesus set an example of serving others
★ understand that disciples serve Jesus and others
★ learn that there are many ways to serve others
★ offer Jesus praise for being Lord

BIBLE BACKGROUND

Think for a moment of Jesus' miracles and the variation we see in them. From calming the sea and changing water to wine to healing lepers and raising Lazarus from death, Jesus performed miracles to serve and help others. Jesus' miracles fell into two main categories: power over nature and power over humanity. But if we look a bit deeper, we recognize "miracles" of love where the spirit triumphed over attitudes and emotions. When Jesus helped and befriended Zacchaeus, it was certainly a miracle of Jesus' love that changed the life of a perpetually cold and selfish man. When Jesus healed Peter's mother-in-law, there was love and caring apparent—even in the way this woman turned to serve Jesus and his friends. Serving others, whether divinely amazing or spiritually loving, was as miraculous as the lessons Jesus taught us about living as serving disciples!

Kids know that it's important to serve others upon occasion, but when serving and discipleship are combined, they recognize a much more committed form of reaching out to Jesus and others. Use this lesson to help kids become aware that discipleship involves not only following Jesus but serving others with gladness and love.

POWER Focus

You'll need foam packing peanuts (or real peanuts in the shell) and plastic spoons for this activity.

As kids arrive, greet them warmly and hand each child a plastic spoon. Invite kids to form three lines and explain that you'll have a lively relay race to see how well kids can serve one another. Then hand the last person in each line two foam packing peanuts. Say:

Place these packing peanuts on your plastic spoons. When I say "go," you'll serve the peanuts to the person ahead of you in line, passing the peanuts from spoon to spoon. Continue serving the peanuts from one person to the next down the line. If a peanut drops, pick it up and go back one person to begin serving again. We'll continue until we've passed the peanuts down the line and back again!

When the relay is finished, have everyone sit in line and ask:

★ **Was serving one another easy or hard? Explain.**
★ **How did you help one another accomplish your serving goal?**
★ **Would your goal have been met if you had given up trying to serve? Why not?**
★ **How is this like the way Jesus serves us? how we should serve others?**

Say: **Serving one another isn't always easy, but if our goal is to help and serve others, we want to keep trying no matter what! Jesus spent his entire life serving and helping others, and he often served them in**

miraculous ways! As disciples, we want to take Jesus' example and
serve others, too.

Today we'll be exploring ways to serve others as Jesus' loving disciples. We'll hear about three miraculous ways Jesus helped other
people. And we'll add the next cool item to our Disciple Kits—so
keep your plastic spoons in a safe place until then! Now let's discover how Jesus served three people in three astounding ways!

THE MIGHTY MESSAGE

Before class, photocopy the Why, What, How? handout from page
124 for each child.

Have kids form pairs or trios and hand each child a handout and a pencil.

Say: **These are check lists that we'll fill out as we read each short Bible
story. We'll see what good detectives you and your part-
ners are as we discover how Jesus served others and
how those people responded to Jesus. I'll read a short
Bible story as you listen for three things: why the
person in the story needed help, what Jesus did to
help that person, and how the person responded to
Jesus' help. Write your answers on your handout.**

**Our first story is about a time when Jesus helped
a disciple's mother-in-law. Listen carefully!** Read
aloud Mark 1:29-31, then ask:

★ **Why did Peter's mother-in-law need Jesus'
help?** (Have kids write "she was sick" or "she had
a fever" on the space.)

★ **What did Jesus do to help her?** (He made her
well.)

★ **How did Peter's mother-in-law respond?** (She
served Jesus and the others.)

Say: **Good for you! Peter's mother-in-law was ill, and
Jesus helped by making her well. And when Jesus served the woman,
she responded by serving, too! Let's see if you can figure out this next
one!**

Read aloud Luke 5:4-7, 10b, 11. Ask:

★ **Why did the fishermen need help?** (They hadn't caught any fish.)

★ **What did Jesus do to help them?** (He made them catch many fish.)

Make a chart of
Jesus' disciples, then
read in the Bible
and record how
they served Jesus
and others.
Challenge kids to
serve in as many of
the same ways
as possible
this week.

★ **How did the men respond to Jesus?** (They followed him; they went to fish for people and bring them to Jesus.)

Say: **Catching all those fish was a real miracle! Jesus served those fishermen in an amazing way, didn't he? And the men responded by following Jesus and going to bring more people to follow him, too. Now let's see if you can do as well on the last story.**

Read aloud Luke 17:11-19, then ask:

★ **Why did the ten lepers need help?** (They were sick; they needed healing.)

★ **What did Jesus do to serve them?** (He cured them; he made them well.)

★ **How did the men respond to Jesus?** (Nine left, but one came back to thank Jesus.)

Say: **Wow! That's a powerful story! Did you notice how only one of the men Jesus helped in this story came back to thank him?** Ask:

★ **How can we respond to Jesus' loving help?**

★ **Why is it important to thank Jesus?**

★ **In what ways can we thank Jesus for his help?**

Say: **There are many ways we can express our thanks and appreciation to Jesus. We can tell him thank-you in a prayer, we can praise God, we can obey Jesus, and we can help Jesus by being kind to others and serving them just as he serves us! In fact, disciples serve Jesus and others as often as they can. So let's leap into serving Jesus right now by learning more about being devoted disciples and adding the next item to our Disciple Kits.**

THE MESSAGE IN MOTION

Before class, purchase opaque paint pens in light and dark skin tones. Opaque paint pens are available at most craft stores. You'll also need felt and fabric scraps, scissors, tacky craft glue, fine-tipped permanent markers, and thick yarn (or fake craft hair) to use for hair, beards, or mustaches. Kids will be making people from the plastic spoons they used in the Power Focus activity. Photocopy the sample faces in the margin and set them out for kids to look at and copy onto their spoon people if they desire.

Set out the craft items and have kids hold their plastic spoons from earlier in the lesson. Say: **We've been learning that disciples serve Jesus and others, just as Jesus did. Think of someone you could serve this week. It might be someone in your family. Or maybe a friend, neighbor, or someone at school needs your help and encouragement. You'll be making spoon people to remind you of someone you can help this week. Then we'll review all the things in our Disciple Kits and what they represent.**

Have kids use the opaque paint pens to color faces on the backs of the plastic spoons. Tell kids the paint will dry in a minute or two if they blow on it. As the spoons dry, let kids decide on what face they'll add to their spoon people and what hairstyle, beard, or mustache they might choose to make. Use fine-tipped permanent markers for facial features and tacky glue to attach hair and fabric clothing. As kids work, have them discuss how serving others is also a wonderful way to serve Jesus and thank him for all he does for us.

When the spoon people are finished, have kids hold them up and tell one way they can serve someone this week. Then tell kids to get their Disciple Kits in order to review the items inside. Say: **You now have six items in your Disciple Kits. Let's review all six disciple truths together. Hold up each item as we repeat its truth.**

   Truth 1: A disciple has faith in God's promises. (PVC pipe)
   Truth 2: A disciple celebrates Jesus. (party horn)
   Truth 3: A disciple learns about God. (phylactery box)
   Truth 4: A disciple trusts Jesus. (boat-in-a-bottle)
   Truth 5: A disciple seeks Jesus. (sunglasses)
   Truth 6: A disciple serves Jesus and others. (spoon person)

Say: **These are important truths to remember, and knowing them will help us be better disciples our whole lives! Something else that will help us be better disciples is learning God's Word and putting it to use in our lives!**

SUPER SCRIPTURE

Gather kids in a group and repeat Philippians 2:10, 11 three times in unison. Then invite volunteers to repeat the verse. If you have older kids, have them also repeat the extra challenge verse.

Say: **Wow! I just love this verse because it speaks of Jesus' power and authority and how everyone will respect and honor Jesus. Just think! At Jesus' name, every knee should bow and tongue confess that he alone is Lord! Only Jesus' name does this—no other name will do. The Bible has another verse that tells of Jesus' name and how he is the only one who can save us from sin. Listen as I read that verse.** Read aloud Acts 4:12, then ask:

★ **How does knowing that Jesus is our Savior help us want to be the best disciples we can be?**

★ **In what ways can this verse encourage us to serve Jesus? to serve others?**

Repeat Philippians 2:10, 11 once more together. Then say: **Let's play a review game to make sure that everyone knows this powerful verse. Form trios, and we'll begin!**

When kids have formed trios, say: **Choose someone to be the knee, someone to be the tongue, and someone to be the Bible book. When I say, "That at the name of Jesus," the knees will kneel and say, "every knee should bow, in heaven and on earth and under the earth." Then the tongues can say, "and every tongue confess that Jesus Christ is Lord, to the glory of God the Father." Then the Bible books can say, "Philippians 2:10, 11." Then we'll switch roles!**

After three repetitions, have kids sit in a circle. Say: **You're doing such a great job learning God's Word! We need to learn God's Word and put it to use in our lives as well. Jesus *is* Lord, and for that we can thank him greatly! Let's offer a prayer thanking Jesus for being our Lord and for showing us how to be serving disciples.**

A POWERFUL PROMISE

Have kids sit in a circle and ask for a moment of silence, then say: **We've learned today that Jesus gave many powerful examples of serving and helping others. We've discovered that disciples serve Jesus and others in many different ways. And we've reviewed the Mighty Memory Verse that teaches us about Jesus' lordship. Philippians 2:10, 11 says** (pause and encourage kids to repeat the verse with you), **"That at the name of Jesus every knee should bow, in heaven and on earth and under the earth, and every tongue confess that Jesus Christ is Lord, to the glory of God the Father."** (Repeat the extra challenge verse if you've been learning it.)

Hold up the Bible and say: **The New Testament is filled with ways that Jesus served others and helped them. Jesus promises to help us, and he asks us to do the same for others. Listen to what Jesus said.** Read aloud John 13:14-17, then continue: **Jesus wants us to be serving, unselfish disciples who help others. Let's make our own special promise to be disciples who serve Jesus and others. When it's your turn, you can say, "I want to serve you and others, Jesus."**

Pass the Bible until everyone has had a chance to make a promise.

Before kids leave, allow five or ten minutes to complete the Whiz Quiz from page 62. If you run out of time, be sure to do this page first thing next week.

Say: **Let's end our time together with the disciple's marching song.** Sing the song to the tune of "The Ants Go Marching One-By-One" and clap on the Xs as you march around the room.

Oh, I'm a disciple of the Lord, hurrah! (XX), *hurrah!* (XX)
Oh, I'm a disciple of the Lord, hurrah! (XX), *hurrah!* (XX)
J-E-S-U-S is his name.
His power and glory I'll always proclaim.
I'm a d-i-s-c-i (XX) *p-l-e* (XX) *that's all I* (XX) *want to be!*
Boom, boom, boom, boom! Boom, boom, boom ... (repeat the song)

End with this responsive good-bye:

Leader: **May you always be a disciple who serves.**

Children: **And also you!**

Distribute the Power Page! take-home papers as kids are leaving. Thank children for coming and encourage them to keep their promises this week.

POWER PAGE!

Sweet Words

Serve God's love to someone special with these adorable and tasty flowers!

You'll need:

★ wrapped swirly candies such as peppermints or saltwater taffy
★ plastic drinking straws
★ construction paper and tape

Serve one another in love.
Galatians 5:13

Directions:

For each flower, tape a candy to one end of a straw. Tear paper leaves and tape them to the straw. Write a Bible verse on a slip of paper and tape it to the flower. Now serve and smile!

Use these verses:

♥ Galatians 5:13   ♥ Romans 5:5
♥ Matthew 25:40   ♥ John 3:16

Thanks, God!

It's important to always praise and thank God! Match the verses with ways to praise, then circle your favorite way to say, "Thanks, God!"

James 4:8	be kind to others
Psalm 119:11	draw near to God
Ephesians 4:32	worship God
Psalm 100:2	learn God's Word

 # MISSING VOWELS

Use the letters a, e, i, o, and u to complete the words to Philippians 2:10, 11.

That at the name of Jesus every knee should bow, in heaven and in earth and under the earth, and every tongue confess that Jesus Christ is Lord, to the glory of God the Father.

WHIZ QUIZ

Color in T (true) or F (false) to answer the questions.

➤ Disciples trust Jesus.   (T)   (F)

➤ Disciples serve Jesus but not others.   (T)   (F)

➤ We can seek Jesus through prayer.   (T)   (F)

➤ Only one leper thanked Jesus for his help.   (T)   (F)

➤ Jesus healed people and made them well.   (T)   (F)

➤ Disciples only have faith in Jesus sometimes.   (T)   (F)

➤ Being a disciple means thinking of others first.   (T)   (F)

WORD BANK

should
heaven
Jesus
earth
tongue
earth
Father
glory

Use the words from the word banks to complete the MIGHTY MEMORY VERSE.

that at the _name_ _of_ _jesus_ every _knee_ _should_ bow, in _heaven_ and on _earth_ and _under_ the _earth_ , and every _tongue_ _confess_ that Jesus _christ_ is _Lord_ to the _glory_ of God the _Father_ .

Philippians 2:10, 11

WORD BANK

That
knee
name
of
confess
under
Christ
Lord

JESUS' PARABLES

I am the way and the
truth and the life. No one
comes to the Father except
through me.
John 14:6

BUILT ON LOVE

Disciples build their lives on Jesus.

Matthew 7:24-27
1 Corinthians 3:10, 11
Psalm 62:6

SESSION SUPPLIES

★ Bibles
★ old blueprints or house plans
★ paper and markers
★ newspapers and craft feathers
★ a brick and paper cups
★ glitter glue and paint pens
★ smooth, medium-sized stones
★ blue first place ribbons and safety pins
★ poster board, tape, and permanent markers
★ photocopies of the Power Page! (page 71)

MIGHTY MEMORY VERSE

I am the way and the truth and the life. No one comes to the Father except through me. John 14:6

SESSION OBJECTIVES

During this session, children will
★ discover that Jesus comes first in our lives
★ understand what "the Lord is our rock" means
★ learn that wise people base their lives on Jesus
★ realize that Jesus has laid a strong foundation for our faith

BIBLE BACKGROUND

Remember the story of the three little pigs? What a great analogy of how we're to build our lives. If we build our lives with solid materials, such as faith in Jesus, trust, forgiveness, kindness, and obedience to God, then no "big bad wolves" can destroy what's been built. But although the story is a wonderful analogy of *how* we're to build our lives, it says nothing about *where* we're to build our lives. For that, we need to turn to Jesus' wonderful parable of the wise and foolish builders, where he talks about the foundations on which two men built their lives. Foundations of money, lies, pride, and human greed will never stand up to the storms that rage through our loves. Only the rock-solid foundation Jesus has laid through his forgiveness and salvation provides an unshakeable base on which we can build strong and sturdy lives. By building our lives on the firm foundation that Jesus has laid, we become modern-day wise men who can weather any storms!

Kids delight in the parable of the wise and foolish builders. After all, anyone can see that building a house on sand puts it in a precarious situation! Through this powerful analogy of what to build our lives on, kids will understand that it's just as foolish to build our lives on shaky foundations that will crumble and erode with troubles. Help kids realize that the only place to build their trust, hope, faith, and very lives is on Jesus and the powerful foundation he has laid for us.

POWER FOCUS

Before class, collect old building blueprints from contractors or architects. Or enlarge and photocopy house building plans from a design book (available at most hardware and home center stores).

As kids arrive, greet them warmly and invite them to look over the building plans. If you have enough copies, invite kids to form small groups to explore the blueprints or plans. Challenge kids to answer in their groups why it's important to have building plans and why it's crucial to find a good building location or solid foundation for the house. If you have time, set out markers and white paper, then invite kids to draw their dream houses.

After about five minutes, call kids together and ask:

★ **Why is it helpful to have building plans for any house or building?**

★ **Why is a firm, sturdy foundation a good base for a building?**

★ **In what ways might the location of a building be a factor?**

Say: **You know, building a house in which to live is very much like building our lives! We want to make sure we have a strong foundation to build on, just as in constructing a house. And we want to make sure what we build our life around is good and solid, just as we want sound building materials for a house.**

Today we'll discover how building our lives on Jesus and his truth is the wise thing to do. We'll learn what makes strong foundations we can rely on. And we'll begin a new Mighty Memory Verse that gives us sound instructions on the best way to build eternal lives in heaven!

But right now, let's hear an exciting story Jesus told about two men who were building houses: one man was very wise, but the other one needed a few building lessons!

THE MIGHTY MESSAGE

Before class, collect a small pile of craft feathers, several newspapers, and a brick. You'll also need three paper cups and markers for this activity. Kids will be reenacting Jesus' parable of the wise and foolish builders.

Have kids form three groups and hand each group a paper cup and one of the following: a pile of feathers, several newspapers, or a brick. Explain that kids will use these props to tell the Bible story. Say:

Jesus told many exciting stories called parables. Parables had important lessons in them, and Jesus knew they were a good way to teach people. Some of the people couldn't understand the stories, but they held great wisdom for those who could! Let's listen to one of Jesus' parables, and you can help tell the story. I'll tell you what to do when we get there!

Once there were two builders who wanted to build houses. One was a very wise builder, and he decided to build his house on solid rock. The other builder built his house on the sand. What do you think happened when it began to rain and rain and rain? Encourage kids to tell their ideas, then continue: **Before we find out what happened then, let's see what happens when _we_ put houses on different kinds of foundations!**

Have the kids with feathers pile them up and place their paper-cup "house" on top. Similarly, have the group with the newspapers shred and pile them up, then put the house on top. Finally, have the group with the brick place their house on top of the brick. Then say: **When I count to three, everyone blow on either the feathers, the papers, or the brick—and we'll see what happens! Ready? One, two, three, blow!** The feathers and papers will blow away and the houses topple over. The brick foundation will stay firm and, if the kids are blowing _only on the brick,_ the house will remain in place.

Say: **Wow! Tell me what happened!** Invite each group to tell what happened to their house and why. Then continue with the story. **It really does matter where and how we build our houses, doesn't it? In Jesus' parable, the man who built his house on the sand had a broken-down**

POWER POINTERS

If your church building has a cornerstone, take kids to see it and remind them that Jesus is the cornerstone of our faith and lives, the foundation that supports the entire structure.

house—it just washed away when troubles came along! But the wise man who built his house on the solid rock found his house safe, sound, and whole when troubles came. Ask:

★ **Which man was wisest? Explain.**

★ **How are the houses in the parable like our lives?** (Help kids see that both houses and lives take time to build and that both will be kept from harm if good materials are put into the building and if both are built on solid ground.)

★ **Why is the foundation we build houses on important?**

★ **Why is the foundation we build our lives on important?**

★ **In what ways is Jesus a solid base for our lives?**

Say: **When we build our trust, faith, hope, and obedience in Jesus and in his truth, we'll live lives that are strong and will keep us from falling when troubles come. Just as houses built on solid rock stand firm when troubles come along, so lives built on Jesus will stand strong. Did you know the Bible tells us that Jesus is the foundation and the Lord is our rock? Listen to what the Bible says!**

Read aloud 1 Corinthians 3:10b, 11; 2 Timothy 2:19a; and Psalm 62:6. Say: **That's pretty awesome! The Lord is our rock, so we will not be shaken. When we build our lives on Jesus, we'll stand firm no matter what may come along. That makes me feel wonderful, how about you? It's so great to be a disciple of Jesus and to discover the ways Jesus helps us be wise! Let's learn more about being wise disciples by adding another piece to our growing Disciple Kits.**

THE MESSAGE IN MOTION

Before class, collect a smooth, medium-sized stone for each child. Kids will be decorating the stones to make neat table decorations or paperweights to remind them that wise disciples build their lives on the rock of Jesus.

Have kids get into pairs or trios and hand each child a smooth stone. Say: **The Bible tells us that the Lord is our strong rock and our sturdy foun-**

dation. **And if we build our lives on him, we will not be shaken. The Bible calls the Lord our rock and our foundation, but it also calls the Lord something else. Listen to this verse and see if you can tell me what else Jesus is called.** Read aloud Ephesians 2:20, 21, then prompt kids to tell you that Jesus is called the chief cornerstone. Explain that a cornerstone helps builders construct a building with walls that are straight and square—in other words, true—which is just what Jesus does for us when we build our lives on him.

Tell kids that they'll be making cornerstones to remind them that disciples build their lives on Jesus and make him the cornerstone of their lives.

Let kids use markers, paint pens, and glitter glue to decorate their stones. As kids work, have them tell ways to make Jesus the foundation of their lives, such as reading the Bible, praying continually, being kind to others, and doing the things Jesus would do.

When the stones are complete, say: **You now have seven items in your Disciple Kits. Let's review all seven disciple truths. Hold up each item as we repeat the truth.**

Truth 1: A disciple has faith in God's promises. (PVC pipe)
Truth 2: A disciple celebrates Jesus. (party horn)
Truth 3: A disciple learns about God. (phylactery box)
Truth 4: A disciple trusts Jesus. (boat-in-a-bottle)
Truth 5: A disciple seeks Jesus. (sunglasses)
Truth 6: A disciple serves Jesus and others. (spoon person)
Truth 7: A disciple builds his life on Jesus. (cornerstone)

Say: **These are such important truths to remember, because knowing them will help us become stronger disciples. Something else that will help us be even more powerful disciples is knowing God's Word! So let's begin a new Mighty Memory Verse that teaches us more about our foundation—Jesus.**

SUPER SCRIPTURE

Before this activity, write John 14:6 on a sheet of paper or newsprint and tape it to the wall or door for kids to read.

Gather kids in front of the verse and read the verse aloud two times. Say: **This verse comes from the Gospel of John, and it tells us two things about Jesus. It tells us that Jesus alone is the way, the truth, and the life.**

And it tells us that the only way to get to God our Father is through Jesus. What do you think this means? Encourage kids to tell their thoughts, then say: **Jesus is our Savior who died for our sins so we could be close to God. Only through Jesus do we have forgiveness, salvation, and the way to God in heaven. That makes this a very important verse, doesn't it?**

Repeat the verse two more times, then say: **We can remember the order of "the way and the truth and the life" by recognizing that those words—*way, truth,* and *life*—come in reverse alphabetical order. That's neat, isn't it? The letter W for *way* is at the end of the alphabet, then back up a bit and you have the letter T for *truth.* Back up even more and you have L for *life.* Who can repeat the first part of the verse without looking at the words?**

Call on volunteers to repeat the first portion of the verse. When everyone who wants a chance has tried, say: **Jesus is giving us building plans in this verse: the right plans to get to our Father in heaven! Building plans are like maps, so let's draw a Scripture map for this verse!**

Tape a large sheet of poster board to the wall or door and help kids create a Scripture map according to the illustration in the margin. Point out that Jesus is the way, the truth, and the life and that he is the only way to get to the Father in heaven. Recite the verse two more times using the Scripture map you just drew.

Say: **That was fun! In fact, learning God's Word can be as fun as it is important. Just think! We've learned that Jesus is the only way to reach our Father in heaven, and that's important to know. Let's offer a prayer of thanks to Jesus for helping show us the plans for drawing near to God and for being the foundation we build our lives on.**

Leave the verse and the Scripture map up for next week.

A POWERFUL PROMISE

Before class, purchase or make a first place blue ribbon for each child. Attach a safety pin at the top of each ribbon for pinning it in place. If you have young children, you may wish to tape the ribbons on their clothing. You'll also need a permanent marker.

Have kids sit in a circle and ask for a moment of silence, then say: **We've learned today that Jesus is our rock and our salvation and that he alone is the cornerstone of our lives. We've discovered that wise disciples build their lives on Jesus. And we've learned that Jesus is the way, the truth, and the life. John 14:6 says** (pause and encourage kids to repeat the verse with you), **"I am the way and the truth and the life. No one comes to the Father except through me."**

Hand each child a blue ribbon and say: **Jesus has promised to be the strong foundation that will enable us to reach the Father and to build strong lives. Let's make our own special promise to make Jesus number one in our lives. For if we keep Jesus in first place, we'll be building a strong foundation in him. We'll pass this pen and take turns saying, "I'll make you first place in my life, Jesus!" Then sign the back of the ribbon and pin it in place.** Continue until everyone has had a chance to make a promise.

Say: **Let's end our time together with the disciple's marching song to show how proud and happy we are to be Jesus' disciples!** Sing to the tune of "The Ants Go Marching One-By-One" and clap on the Xs as you march around the room two times.

Oh, I'm a disciple of the Lord, hurrah! (XX), *hurrah!* (XX)
Oh, I'm a disciple of the Lord, hurrah! (XX), *hurrah!* (XX)
J-E-S-U-S is his name.
His power and glory I'll always proclaim.
I'm a d-i-s-c-i (XX) *p-l-e* (XX) *that's all I* (XX) *want to be!*
Boom, boom, boom, boom! Boom, boom, boom ... (repeat the song)

End with this responsive good-bye:
Leader: **May you build your lives on Jesus.**
Children: **And also you!**
Distribute the Power Page! take-home papers as kids are leaving. Thank children for coming and encourage them to keep their promises this week.

POWER PAGE!

BUILDING A BASE

Jesus Is ...

In John 14:6 we learn that Jesus is the way, truth, and life. What else is Jesus? Read the verses and fill in the blanks.

John 8:12   ◯ _ _ _ _

Philippians 2:11   ◯ _ _ _

1 Timothy 4:10   _ _ ◯ _ _ _ _

Micah 5:5   _ ◯ _ _ _

What else is Jesus? Read the circled letters downward.

What's most important in your life? Write or draw your priorities in the boxes.

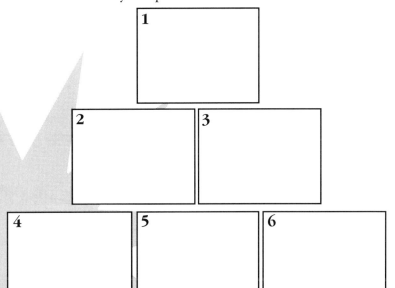

ARE JESUS AND GOD YOUR #1 PRIORITY?

Crazy Circuit Board

Follow the arrows to plug in the missing letters from John 14:6.

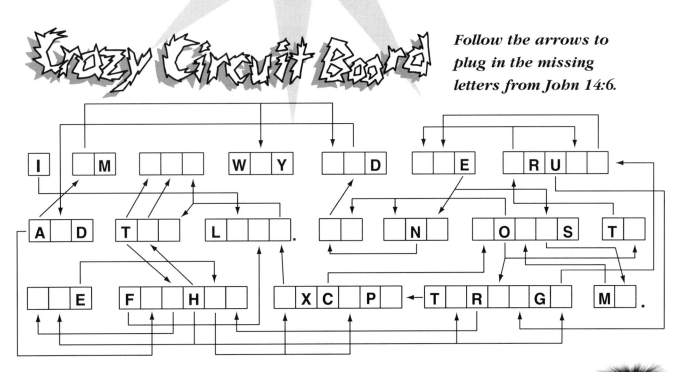

LOST AND FOUND

A disciple encourages others to stay close to God.

Luke 15:8-10
1 Thessalonians 5:11
2 Thessalonians 2:16

SESSION SUPPLIES

★ Bibles
★ coins and envelopes
★ crayons and paper
★ scissors and tape
★ construction paper
★ an empty can
★ photocopies of the Scripture dollar (page 125)
★ photocopies of the Power Page! (page 79)

MIGHTY MEMORY VERSE

I am the way and the truth and the life. No one comes to the Father except through me. John 14:6

(For older kids, add in 1 John 2:6: "Whoever claims to live in him must walk as Jesus did.")

SESSION OBJECTIVES

During this session, children will
★ understand God wants us to be near him
★ realize that Jesus helped others stay close to God
★ explore ways to draw near to God
★ discover how to encourage others to stay near God

BIBLE BACKGROUND

97 . . . 98 . . . 99 . . . 100! Here I come, ready or not! Ah, the sounds of childhood games filled with light-hearted fun and frolic. Hide-and-Seek is a great kids game, but it quickly loses its appeal when the stakes are for real! Being lost from God and wandering from his care through disobedience, neglect, and a host of other sins that sidetrack us isn't fun at all, and it causes God and us great unhappiness. We take great comfort in the fact that God doesn't leave us. Oh, that we were as faithful to God as he is to us! In fact, we're the ones who may leave his side and become wanderers in our own self-imposed wilderness. But God loves us enough to send out the troops to bring us home! Friends, family members, church leaders, and even strangers may help us find our way home to God and his loving embrace in often miraculous ways! It's comforting to know that "neither height nor depth, nor anything else in all creation, will be able to separate us from the love of God that is in Christ Jesus our Lord" (Romans 8:39).

Kids know all too well the dangers of wandering away and becoming lost at a mall or a county fair, but they need help recognizing the incredibly worse danger of wandering away from God. Use this lesson to help kids realize that they need to stay near to God and that Jesus will help them stay ever close to the God who always stays close to them.

POWER focus

Before class, collect ten coins for each child, such as nine shiny pennies and a nickel. At the end of class, this money will be donated to a collection fund that will continue over the next several weeks. Place nine of the coins in an envelope for each child, then hide the extra coins. During the lesson, kids will be counting their nine coins, then seeking their missing tenth.

As kids arrive, greet them and hand each an envelope containing nine coins. When everyone has an envelope, say: **These envelopes are pretend banks, and each of you has ten coins in your bank. Count your coins to be sure.** Pause as kids count their coins and react to the fact they have only nine coins. Then say: **Oh my! I guess some of your coins are lost! See if you can hunt for your missing coins in the room. As soon as you have each found a lost coin, come back and sit down.**

When everyone has found a missing coin, say: **Well, it appears that you were good seekers! But why were you so worried when you were missing only one coin? You had nine others, so why was one coin so important?** Pause for kids to respond, then ask:

★ **What's it like to be lost? to be found after you've been lost?**

★ **Do you think we can be lost from God? Explain.**

★ **How do you think God feels when we become lost and far away from him?**

★ **How do you think God feels when he finds us and we draw near to him?**

Say: **Today we'll be learning about being lost and found and what Jesus has to teach about that. We'll discover how disciples can encourage others to stay close to God. And we'll review our Mighty Memory**

Verse that teaches us about the way to heaven and how Jesus helps us find God. Be sure to hold on to your envelope and ten coins because you'll need them throughout the lesson. Right now, you can help retell today's Bible story, which is about a woman who lost something of great value.

THE **MIGHTY** MESSAGE

Have kids sit in a circle and hold up a coin. Say: **We'll tell the story as we play a game of Who Has the Coin? I'll tell a bit of the story as you pass the coin around the circle. When I say, "Stop the story," I'll choose someone to guess who has the coin. If that person is right, she can answer the question and take the coin. But if she's wrong, the person with the coin answers. Then we'll continue the story and passing the coin. This is another of Jesus' parables that has a wonderful message. See if you can figure out why Jesus told this story.**

Begin passing the coin and telling the story from Luke 15:8-10. Say: **Once there was a woman who had ten shiny coins. She would count her coins every day just to make sure they were all there. Stop the story.** Choose a child to guess who has the coin. If he's right, have him answer the following question. If he's wrong, have the child holding the coin answer. Ask:

★ **How do you know the coins were precious to the woman?**

After the question has been answered, continue the story and passing the coin. Say: **Yes, the coins were precious to the woman. Then one day something awful happened! She counted only nine coins, and she was very worried! Stop the story.** Ask:

★ **Why do you think the woman was worried?**

Continue: **Just as she feared, the woman was missing a coin, and she wanted to find it very badly. Stop the story.** Ask:

★ **What do you think the woman did then?**

Say: **The woman looked everywhere! She lit her lamp and swept the floor and checked behind her big front door, checked beneath the woven rug—she even moved a lady bug! Stop the story.** Ask:

POWER POINTERS

Make pudding and let kids hide chocolate coins in their treats, then search for the hidden treasures with spoons, clean craft sticks, or plastic forks.

★ **Why did the woman look so hard for one missing coin?**

Continue: **Then the woman spied her coin! She picked it up and jumped for joy. Then she ran to tell her friends that her lost coin was found. Stop the story.** Ask:

★ **Why was the woman so happy?**

Say: **The woman was happy because she found what was lost. In the same way, God is happy when even one sinner finds his love and Jesus' forgiveness. Stop the story.**

★ **Why is God happy when someone finds him?**

Say: **You did a great job helping tell this special parable. Do you think you know the important message of this parable?** Allow kids to share their thoughts, then say: **Jesus wanted us to know how precious each of us is to God and how much God wants us close to him. Sometimes we wander away from God and disobey him. But Jesus wants us to know that God will send help so we'll return to him. In fact, that help may be another person—a disciple like you!** Ask:

★ **Why is it important to stay close to God?**

★ **How can we encourage others to stay near to God?** (Lead kids to suggest ways such as helping others by being kind, reminding them to pray, praying for them, and reading the Bible with others.)

Say: **Disciples know that being close to God is the only place to be, so they encourage and help others remain close to God, too. Let's make the next part of our Disciple Kits to remind us that disciples rejoice when we help others find God.**

THE MESSAGE IN **MOTION**

Have kids form pairs or trios and hand each child a sheet of paper. Show kids how to place a coin under the paper and rub across the coin with the side of a crayon. The coin's outline and raised portions will show through the paper and make a print. Encourage kids to make unusual designs and to try different color combinations with their rubbings.

As kids work, have them discuss ways to stay close to God, such as following Jesus, learning from the Bible and God's Word, and prayer. Ask questions such as "What happens when we become lost or wander away from God?"

and "How is this like the way it feels when we get lost from our parents and other people we love?"

When the pictures are complete, have kids display their handiwork.

Then say: **Just as our papers were so close to the coins that they took on the appearance of the coins, we want to remain so close to Jesus that everyone will know that we are his disciples. These coin rubbings can help remind us that being close to Jesus is a precious gift we never want to lose.**

Have kids put their rubbings in their Disciple Kits, then say: **You have eight items in your Disciple Kits. Let's review all the items and the eight truths that they stand for!**

Truth 1: A disciple has faith in God's promises. (PVC pipe)
Truth 2: A disciple celebrates Jesus. (party horn)
Truth 3: A disciple learns about God. (phylactery box)
Truth 4: A disciple trusts Jesus. (boat-in-a-bottle)
Truth 5: A disciple seeks Jesus. (sunglasses)
Truth 6: A disciple serves Jesus and others. (spoon person)
Truth 7: A disciple builds his life on Jesus. (cornerstone)
Truth 8: A disciple helps others stay close to God. (coin rubbings)

Say: **Such beautiful coins rubbings you've made! But nothing is as beautiful to God as when people who are lost from him find him and accept Jesus into their lives! All of heaven rejoices with gladness! There are many ways to stay close to God, and as Jesus' disciples, we can help and encourage others so they'll remain close to God, too. Listen to what the Bible says about encouraging others.**

Read aloud 1 Thessalonians 5:11 and 2 Thessalonians 2:16. Then say: **Jesus shows us ways to stay close to God, and one of these ways is by learning God's Word. Let's review our Mighty Memory Verse and discover the true way to find our Father in heaven.**

SUPER SCRIPTURE

Before class, photocopy the Scripture dollar on page 125 on green paper. Copy and cut out a Scripture dollar for each child. To save time in class, you may want to cut the oval centers from the dollars prior to class. Also, make sure you have a copy of the Mighty Memory Verse (John 14:6) still hanging on the wall or door for kids to read. If you have older kids, add the extra challenge verse if you plan to work on it as well.

Gather kids by the verse and read it aloud in unison three times. Then say: **Do you remember what two things this verse teaches us?** Invite kids to answer, then say: **This verse teaches us that Jesus is the way, the truth, and the life—in reverse alphabetical order—and that the only way to the Father is through Jesus. In other words, this verse teaches us that Jesus is the way to life** (point to the words *way* and *life* on the paper) **and also the way to the Father** (point to the words *comes* and *Father*). **That's very important to remember: Jesus is the way to life and the way to the Father!**

Challenge pairs of kids to repeat the verse without looking at the paper. If they need help, have them call on someone to help out, then let them choose their replacements for the next repetition. Continue until everyone who would like a turn has had one.

Say: **This verse is so important and worth more than any amount of coins or money! But to make it fun to remember, let's use these Scripture dollars and play a game with partners.**

Hand each child a bill and help kids cut the centers out if you haven't done so already. Then say: **You'll each need one of your coins, the Scripture dollar, and a friend. Take turns repeating the verse and having your partner hold the dollar. When you correctly repeat the verse, toss or flip a coin and try to get it through the hole in the dollar. When the coin goes through, both partners can hop up and shout, "Thank you, Jesus, for being the way to God!"**

After several minutes, have kids set their coins and pretend dollars aside. Say: **Learning God's Word is fun and very important, but it's not enough just to repeat God's Word; we need to put God's Word to use in our lives. We've learned that Jesus is the way to life and to heaven, so let's thank Jesus in a prayer for helping us remain close to God.**

A POWERFUL PROMISE

Before class, make a bank from an empty tin can. Cut a strip of construction paper as a label and tape it around the can. Add the words "Find a Coin . . . Help the Lost!" You'll also need crayons for this activity.

Have kids sit in a circle and hold their Scripture dollars. Ask for a moment of silence, then say: **We have learned today that each of us is important to God and that God wants all of us to stay close to him. We've discovered that disciples can help and encourage others to draw near to and find God. And we've reviewed the Mighty Memory Verse that says** (pause and encourage kids to repeat the verse with you), **"I am the way and the truth and the life. No one comes to the Father except through me."** If you have older kids, repeat the extra challenge verse, too.

Say: **Jesus loves us so much and wants us to stay near to God. Jesus also wants us to help others find God. Let's make a special promise to be an encouragement and help to those seeking God. We can say, "I want to help others find you, God" as we pass around these crayons. Then write one word of encouragement on your Scripture dollar.** Continue until everyone has had a chance to make a promise and write a word on the Scripture dollar. Then close with a prayer thanking Jesus for providing the way to God and for helping us remain near to him.

Say: **I challenge you to give your Scripture dollar away to someone this week and to tell that person about God's love, Jesus' forgiveness, or how to stay close to God every day through prayer, reading the Bible, and obeying God.**

Hold up the Find a Coin can. Say: **Now let's think about the coins we've been using today. One way we can help and encourage others is by donating our extra coins to help buy food, clothing, or Bibles. I'll pass this "Find a Coin ... Help the Lost" can around the circle. You can donate your coins from today's lesson, then see if you can find or earn a coin to bring in next week to add to our can. We'll keep collecting money for the next several weeks, then we'll donate the coins to a missions cause to help the lost find God.** Pass the can and have kids drop in their coins, then set the can on a table for next week.

End with this responsive good-bye:

Leader: **May you always remain close to God!**

Children: **And also you!**

Distribute the Power Page! take-home papers as kids are leaving. Thank children for coming and encourage them to keep their promises this week.

POWER PAGE!

LOST-n-FOUND

Read these short Bible stories of important things and people who were lost then found. Match the stories with what was found!

2 Kings 22:1-10   a prophet!

Luke 15:8-10   a lost sheep!

Jonah 1:1–2:10   a scroll that
                                     was God's Word!

Luke 15:3-7   a coin!

Shadow Shade

Make this cool lampshade and, as you watch the shadows, think of how Jesus stays as close as our shadows.

Directions:
Purchase an inexpensive lampshade (or check your attic or garage sales). Using a pin, poke designs in the shade. Make bigger holes for bigger shadows. When you turn your lamp on in a dark room, you'll see your design dance on the walls. Cool!

SCRAMBLER

Unscramble the words in the word bank to complete John 14:6.

I am the WAY and the TRUTH and the LIFE. No one COMES to the FATHER except THROUGH ME.

John 14:6

WORD BANK

ouhtgrb   em

yaw   smeco

thraFe   bturt

efil   eht

Lesson 9

ONE WAY

A disciple obeys God.

Matthew 7:13, 14
Acts 4:12
Ephesians 2:8, 9

SESSION SUPPLIES

★ Bibles
★ colored and white poster board
★ markers and scissors
★ masking tape and glue
★ glitter glue and sequins
★ photocopies of the traffic signs (page 125)
★ photocopies of the Whiz Quiz (page 88) and the Power Page! (page 87)

MIGHTY MEMORY VERSE

I am the way and the truth and the life. No one comes to the Father except through me. John 14:6
(For older kids, add in 1 John 2:6: "Whoever claims to live in him must walk as Jesus did.")

SESSION OBJECTIVES

During this session, children will
★ discover that Jesus obeyed God
★ learn that there's only one way to God
★ discover how to stay on the right path to God
★ thank Jesus for providing a way to heaven

BIBLE BACKGROUND

Traffic tickets for going the wrong direction on a one-way street aren't much fun. But when a traffic rule is disobeyed, a fine encourages us not to repeat the offense. Taking a turn down the wrong path in our Christian walk, however, can have much more dire consequences! And a simple fine would seem glorious when compared to the destruction, desolation, and depression we might find at the end of the wrong path and the wide road that the Bible warns against taking. It's vital that we heed the "traffic signs" that Jesus provides for us as disciples—signs such as following his example of learning Scripture, obeying God, and making solid choices that keep us traveling in the right direction toward our heavenly Father. The road isn't always paved and has its share of bumps and barriers, but it is always worth the trip! And when we finally burst through that narrow heavenly gate, we can enter God's courts with thanksgiving and praise for a road well traveled!

Kids need to realize that there are many paths in life to choose from—but only one that leads to God! With the sound warning from Matthew 7:13, 14 kids can begin to understand that going down wrong paths can have eternal consequences. Help kids discover the true way to God with this lively lesson about obedience and paths.

POWER FOCUS

Before class, use colored poster board and markers to make the following traffic signs: Stop, One Way, Yield, Go, and Do Not Enter. Use the signs on page 125 as patterns. You'll also need to place masking-tape paths on the floor. Make one straight path from one end of the room to the other. Then make other paths that are winding, circular, or zigzagged. Be sure the lines all connect at one end of the straight path so kids can go in many different directions around the room but only one way leads to the straight path.

As kids arrive, greet them and motion where to sit using the One Way and Stop signs. Then say: **There are lots of signs we see to direct traffic on the streets. What are these signs, and what do they mean?** Hold up the signs and allow kids to tell what each sign is and what it means. Then name other signs such as Railroad Crossing, Walk, and No Parking.

Say: **Let's use these signs to play a game. Find a partner and a place to begin along one of the paths. Decide who will be the first leader and who will be the follower. The leader will guide the follower around the paths until I say, "switch." Then switch places and we'll continue. Be sure to keep your eyes on the traffic signs!**

Have kids travel in any direction they'd like as you flash signs. Have kids respond to the One Way sign by moving in whatever direction you point the arrow. After a few minutes, have kids switch roles and continue for a bit longer. Then have kids go on "solo trips," traveling the roads without their partners.

Flash the Stop sign and direct kids to sit in a group. Then ask:

★ **Did you obey the traffic signs? Why or why not?**

★ **Which was easier: having someone to go along the paths with you or going alone? Explain.**

★ **Which path was easiest to follow? Why?**

★ **In what ways was this activity like following Jesus along the path to God?**

Say: **The Bible tells us there are many paths in life, but only one leads to God. Today we'll discover which path leads to God and how to stay on that right path. We'll be learning more about being disciples who obey the Lord and follow him. And we'll review our Mighty Memory Verse that tells us how to get to God. Right now, let's learn a bit more about paths and which is the right path and which are the wrong paths to choose!**

POWER POINTERS

Have kids use their sign cutouts in a collage and write good disciple tips below each, such as "Stop" and obey God!

THE MIGHTY MESSAGE

Before class, photocopy and enlarge the traffic signs from page 125. Make one copy for each child.

Hand each child a page of traffic signs and have kids quickly color and cut out the signs. Then say: **You can use your traffic signs to help tell about the Bible passages we'll be reading. When I ask you "Which sign?" hold up the sign that you think works. For example, if we're talking about worshiping sports heroes, the signs you'd want to flash would be Stop or Do Not Enter because we're not to worship or follow anyone but Jesus. If I read about the right path to God, you'll want to hold up Go or One Way to show that this is the right way to go. Ready? Then here we go! Which sign?** Pause for kids to hold their Go signs, then say: **Good for you! Now let's hear what the Bible says about finding the right path to God.**

Sometimes we get caught up in making money and seeing how rich we can get! We might even think money and possessions are the paths to heaven. But the Bible says ... (read aloud Matthew 6:19, 24). **Which sign?** Pause for kids to hold up their Stop or Do Not Enter signs. Ask kids to explain their choices, then continue: **Well, money and possessions aren't**

the way to heaven! But some people think that getting to heaven is easy. They say, "I haven't done anything really wrong, such as robbing a bank or hurting anyone. Of course I'll get to heaven!" But listen: (read aloud Acts 4:12). **Which sign?** Pause for kids to hold up their Stop or Do Not Enter signs.

Ask for explanations of their choices, then continue: **Well, we can't find God through ourselves, but how about finding God through the wonderful things we do? Let's see!** Read aloud Ephesians 2:8, 9, then ask: **Which sign?** Again, have kids tell why they chose the sign they held up. Say: **Wow! We're not on the right path to God yet, but maybe this will help us!** Read aloud Matthew 7:13, 14, then ask: **Which sign for the wide gate?** Pause as kids hold up the Stop and Do Not Enter signs. Then ask: **Which sign for the narrow gate?** Have kids hold up their Go or One Way signs.

Say: **This verse tells us that there are two gates: one that is wide and that leads to evil, and one that is narrow and that leads to God.** Ask:

★ **Why do more people go through the wide gate?**

★ **Why is the narrow gate hard to find?**

★ **Which is better: to go the easy, wrong way or the more difficult but right way? Why?**

Say: **The Bible warns us that the way to happiness and eternal life may not be easy, but it's sure worth it! And that's the gate and the path we want to be on, isn't it? Listen to one more verse, then flash an appropriate sign.** Read aloud John 14:6 and lead kids in flashing their One Way, Yield, or Go signs.

Say: **Hooray for you! We've finally found the one path to God, and it's through Jesus our Lord! When we stay on the right path with Jesus, we'll reach our Father in heaven!** Ask:

★ **What helps us stay on the right path to God?** (Suggestions might include reading the Bible, obeying God, being baptized, following Jesus, and praying.)

★ **Why is it so important to stay on the right path to God?**

Say: **When we obey traffic signs, we reach our destinations safely. And when we accept Jesus into our lives and obey him through prayer, baptism, reading the Bible, and being kind to others, we reach our heavenly destination! That's pretty awesome and very important. Disciples obey the Lord and stay on the right path that leads to heaven. Let's make one more item for our Disciple Kits as we learn more about the way to God.**

THE MESSAGE IN **MOTION**

Before class, cut rectangular pieces of white poster board to fit the One Way signs. Kids will glue the signs to the poster board, then cut around the signs.

Set the poster board, scissors, glitter glue, glue, and sequins on a table. You may wish to cover the table with newspapers. Invite kids to work in pairs or trios and explain that they'll be embellishing their One Way signs to put in the Disciple Kits to show that there's only one way to God.

Have kids glue their One Way signs to poster-board rectangles, then cut out the signs. Use markers to strike out the word *one* and write the word *only* above it in capital letters to symbolize that Jesus isn't just one way to God—he's the only way to God! Then use sequins and glitter glue to embellish the signs and really make them shine! As kids work, discuss why it's important for disciples to stay on the straight path to heaven by following and obeying Jesus.

When the signs are complete, say: **These signs are super! And now you have nine items in your Disciple Kits. Let's review all nine disciple truths together. Hold up each item as we repeat the truth.**

Truth 1: A disciple has faith in God's promises. (PVC pipe)

Truth 2: A disciple celebrates Jesus. (party horn)

Truth 3: A disciple learns about God. (phylactery box)

Truth 4: A disciple trusts Jesus. (boat-in-a-bottle)

Truth 5: A disciple seeks Jesus. (sunglasses)

Truth 6: A disciple serves Jesus and others. (spoon person)

Truth 7: A disciple build his life on Jesus. (cornerstone)

Truth 8: A disciple helps others stay close to God. (coin rubbings)

Truth 9: A disciple obeys God. (sign)

Say: **What important truths to remember! And knowing them will help us be better disciples our whole lives through! The only way to God is through Jesus, and one way to follow Jesus is to learn God's Word, just as Jesus did! Let's review our Mighty Memory Verse and what it teaches us about the only way to heaven!**

SUPER SCRIPTURE

Be sure you have the Mighty Memory Verse (John 14:6) hanging on the wall or door for kids to read.

Repeat the Mighty Memory Verse three times in unison, then invite pairs of kids to repeat the verse. Have one child say the first portion and her partner repeat the second half. If you have older kids, have them form trios and add in the extra challenge verse, too.

Say: **You're learning God's Word so well! It's not easy all the time, but nothing is more worth it! Even Jesus learned Scripture, and disciples naturally want to do the things that Jesus did. We've been learning what this verse means—now let's explore how this verse helps us in our lives.** Ask:

★ **How does it help to know that Jesus is the only way to God?**

★ **In what ways does knowing this affect our choices? how we obey God? how we follow Jesus?**

★ **How can we help others know that Jesus is the way, truth, and life?**

Say: **We know that we can't get to God through money or what we do or how good we are. The only way is through knowing, loving, and following Jesus. True disciples follow the straight path of Jesus' example by being baptized, learning God's Word, and obeying the Father. That's what keeps us on the right path to God! Now let's play a game using the straight path in our room. We'll take turns hopping, walking, tiptoeing, or walking backwards down the path and repeating the Mighty Memory Verse. When you reach the other end, we'll cheer and give each other high fives!**

Continue walking the straight path and repeating the verse until everyone has had a turn and given a high five. Then say: **The Bible tells us that the wide gate leads to evil, and many people find that gate the easiest to go through. We want to enter by the narrow gate, which isn't always the easiest. Jesus knew that! And Jesus promises to help us stay on the straight path and find the narrow gate to everlasting life. What a wonderful thing when we go through that beautiful gate! Let's share a prayer thanking Jesus for being the only way to God and for helping us be disciples who obey God. Then we'll see how we're to enter God's gates!**

A POWERFUL PROMISE

You'll need the Find a Coin bank from last week.

Have kids sit in a circle and hold their Bibles, then say: **We've been learning about being Jesus' disciples for several weeks now, and you're all doing so well. We've learned a lot just today! We've discovered that disciples obey God and follow Jesus on the straight path to God. We've learned that the way is narrow and that it isn't always easy, but that finding our way to God through Jesus is worth it! And we've reviewed the Mighty Memory Verse that teaches us the true way to God. Let's say John 14:6 together.** Repeat the Mighty Memory Verse and the extra challenge verse, if you've worked on it.

Say: **For our prayer today, let's read a wonderful Psalm from the Bible about how we can enter God's gates—that narrow gate we read about today. Scooch next to someone you're sitting beside and we'll take turns reading lines in pairs. When we reach the end of the Psalm, we'll say "amen."**

Read aloud Psalm 100. The Psalm has eleven lines, so this will accommodate twenty-two kids if they're in pairs. Have each pair read a line, then end with a corporate "amen." If kids brought coins for the Find a Coin bank, have them donate their offerings at this time.

Say: **Wasn't that beautiful? We're to enter God's gates with thanksgiving, praise, gladness, and songs. Let's express our commitment to be the best disciples we can be by entering God's gates with singing! We can sing our disciple's marching song as we praise and honor God.**

Sing the words of the song on page 60 to the tune of "The Ants Go Marching One-By-One," clapping on the Xs.

Before kids leave, allow five or ten minutes to complete the Whiz Quiz from page 88. If you run out of time, be sure to do this page first thing next week.

End with this responsive good-bye:

Leader: **May you always obey God.**

Children: **And also you!**

Distribute the Power Page! take-home papers as kids are leaving. Thank children for coming and encourage them to keep their commitment to stay on the right path this week.

POWER PAGE!

Sign Up!

Make a cool mobile for your room!

Draw traffic signs on poster board and color and cut them out. (Be sure to color the backs of the signs, too!)

Use fishing line to hang your signs from a drinking straw, ruler, or clothes hanger. Hang your mobile from your ceiling and think how each sign could help us follow Jesus.

OUTTA THIS WORLD!

SLICK TRICK

Write the word *live* and an arrow pointing to the *right* on an index card. Hold the card up to a mirror and look at the word. If we don't obey God and stay on the *right* path to him, we can get turned around and find this. How can the **MIGHTY MEMORY VERSE** help us stay on the *right* path?

live →	← evil

Seek-n-Search

T	H	E	L	I	F	E
S	A	N	D	I	A	M
T	O	T	R	U	T	H
X	T	H	E	V	H	A
C	V	R	X	M	E	N
O	Z	O	C	O	R	D
M	T	U	E	N	O	W
E	H	G	P	E	Z	A
S	E	H	T	H	E	Y

All the words from the Mighty Memory Verse are hidden in this puzzle. After you circle a word in the puzzle, cross it out below.

I am the way and the truth and the life. No one comes to the Father except through me. (John 14:6)

WHIZ QUIZ

Color in YES or NO to answer each question.

✴ A parable is a story with a lesson.   (YES) (NO)

✴ We want our families to be first in our lives.   (YES) (NO)

✴ Wise people don't need to build their lives on Jesus.   (YES) (NO)

✴ Jesus is our strong foundation.   (YES) (NO)

✴ Disciples don't worry about encouraging others.   (YES) (NO)

✴ Even Jesus obeyed God.   (YES) (NO)

✴ Jesus is the only way to God.   (YES) (NO)

AIM THE ARROWS

Draw arrows to place the words in their correct positions to complete the Mighty Memory Verse. The first word has been done for you.

way   life   the   am   one

the

I am the way the truth and the life No, one comes to the father except through me,

John 14:6

the

and

comes   through   except   to   the

and   truth   No   Father   me

JESUS' DEATH & RESURRECTION

For God so loved the world
that he gave his one and only
Son, that whoever believes in
him shall not perish but have
eternal life.
John 3:16

Disciples love others.

Matthew 26:26-30
John 13:35; 15:12

SESSION SUPPLIES

★ Bibles
★ bread and fruit juice
★ paper cups, plastic knives, and spoons
★ pitted dates and cream cheese
★ green construction paper
★ scissors, markers, and glue
★ a bowl of water and paper towels
★ laundry detergent flakes
★ a mixer and bowl
★ aluminum foil and thick twine
★ poster board and tape
★ photocopies of the rebus patterns (page 126)
★ photocopies of the Power Page! (page 97)

THE LAST SUPPER

MIGHTY MEMORY VERSE

For God so loved the world that he gave his one and only Son, that whoever believes in him shall not perish but have eternal life. John 3:16

SESSION OBJECTIVES

During this session, children will
★ understand that Jesus loved his disciples and us
★ realize that Jesus served his disciples with love
★ discover that disciples love others as they love Jesus
★ thank Jesus for his gift of everlasting love

BIBLE BACKGROUND

In John 13:35 Jesus makes it very clear how others will know we are disciples: "if you love one another." It's often much easier said than done to love others, especially those who seem different or who have a mean attitude or are otherwise "unlovable." And it's just as easy to fall into the trap of calling ourselves Christians and disciples in word but not modeling Jesus' acceptance or love through our actions. After all, Jesus warned, what gain is it to only love those who love us? Disciples of Jesus take the challenge to love even the most unlovable among us and treat them as if they were the Lord. By modeling Christ's love to others and genuinely caring about that hungry stranger or forgiving the hardened headline criminal, we begin to nurture the heart of Christ, not just in our own lives, but in the hearts of others!

Kids may find one of the toughest areas in which to obey Jesus is in loving others, especially playground bullies and classroom ruffians. But once children understand that Jesus has love enough for everyone, they begin to realize they may have a bit more love to go around themselves! Use this special lesson to help kids see the examples of love Jesus set for us to follow and then pass on his love to others as his loving disciples.

POWER FOCUS

Before class, purchase a small loaf of shepherd's bread or French bread. You'll also need pitted dates, softened cream cheese, and fruit juice.

As kids arrive, greet them warmly and have them form three groups. Assign one group to be the table-setters, one to be the date-stuffers, and one to be the leaf-makers. Instruct the date-stuffers to use plastic knives to gently open dates sideways, then to spread cream cheese inside. Place the dates on a paper towel. Have the leaf-makers make large green construction-paper palm fronds by cutting oval-shaped leaves and fringing the sides with scissors. And have the table-setters collapse the legs of a table and place it on the floor. Then have them set a place for each person with paper towels and small paper cups.

As kids work, explain that today you're going to hold a celebration of love by following a special example Jesus set for us one night at dinner. Ask kids to tell about loving things they've done for others and how it made them feel. When the table, dates, and leaves are finished, have kids gather in a group. Ask:

★ **Why do you think love is such an important thing to feel and to give others?**

★ **What would the world be like without love, giving, sharing, and caring?**

★ **Why is Jesus a good example to follow if we want to learn about love?**

Say: **Jesus spent his entire life teaching and loving others. And as his powerful disciples, we want to love as Jesus loved and treat others in the same way. Today we'll discover how Jesus showed his first disciples love and how he encouraged them to love others. We'll learn what it takes to love others as we love Jesus. And we'll begin a new Mighty Memory Verse that tells us about God's love for us.**

Right now, let's go back in time and discover what Jesus did for his disciples during one very special meal they shared.

THE **MIGHTY** MESSAGE

Before this activity, have a bowl of water and paper towels handy.

Hand each child a paper palm frond and say: **One day long ago, the people of Jerusalem were very excited. Jesus was coming to town! And when they saw him approach riding on a donkey, they waved palm fronds, which were a symbol of victory.** **"Hosanna!" they cried! "Blessed is he who comes in the name of the Lord" Then they followed Jesus into the city.** Have kids wave the paper leaves and walk once around the room shouting, "Hosanna! Blessed is he who comes in the name of the Lord." Then direct kids to sit on their leaves like mats.

Before the night of Passover, Jesus told his disciples to prepare a dinner for him and his disciples to share. Let's gather around our table and share a prayer thanking Jesus for his love. Lead kids to the table and have them find places to sit on the floor. Invite kids to use their paper leaves as placemats. Then pray: **Dear Lord, we thank you for the great love you give us each day. Please help us follow your loving example. Amen.** Have kids nibble the stuffed dates as you ask:

★ **How did the people waving the palm fronds honor and praise Jesus?**

★ **In what ways can we honor and praise Jesus?**

Continue the story: **As the disciples were sharing the meal, Jesus took bread and wine and blessed them. He shared both with his disciples and asked that they eat and drink them as they remembered him. This was Jesus' way of sharing his body, heart, and life with them. Jesus also promised that they'd share the meal again in heaven. We still celebrate the bread and wine; we call it Communion or the Lord's Supper.** Let kids have a bit of bread and fruit juice as you ask:

POWER POINTERS

Have a church leader explain your church's tradition of the Lord's Supper. Be sure to let kids ask questions and express how they feel knowing that Jesus gave us this special meal.

★ How did Jesus express his love through sharing the bread and wine?

★ How does Jesus' promise of sharing bread and wine in heaven show his love to us?

Say: **When they were finished eating, Jesus got up from the table and did a remarkable thing. He washed his disciples' feet! To show how Jesus served his disciples, I'm going to wash your hands.** Wash each child's hands with a bit of water, then dry the hands with the paper towels. When you're finished, say: **Jesus demonstrated his love by serving his disciples, and he also told them to serve one another just as he had served them.** Ask:

★ **How does serving others demonstrate our love for them? for Jesus?**

★ **What are ways you could serve someone today?**

Say: **When the meal and the foot-washing were over, Jesus went to pray for his disciples, for us, and for himself, for he was about to face a very hard time that we will learn about next week.**

During the Last Supper, Jesus demonstrated his love through sharing a meal and the bread and wine. He also demonstrated his love by serving his disciples and by praying for others. Jesus wants all of his disciples—not just the twelve disciples who ate with him but all of us—to love others as he loved us! Listen to two beautiful verses that Jesus spoke. Read aloud John 15:12 and 13:35. **Jesus tells us that we're to love others as he loves us. If we do, all people will know that we are Jesus' disciples.**

Now let's make a fun item for your Disciple Kits that will remind us how Jesus showed his love through serving his disciples.

THE MESSAGE IN MOTION

Before class, purchase a box of laundry detergent flakes. When they're mixed with a bit of water, they become dough-like. You'll also need an electric or hand mixer, water, plastic spoons, a bowl, thick twine, scissors, and aluminum foil. To save time, cut the twine into one 12-inch length for each child.

Hand each child a square of aluminum foil and a piece of twine. Explain that you'll be making soap-on-a-rope to remind you of how Jesus washed his disciples' feet as a demonstration of his love.

Pour half a box of soap flakes into the mixing bowl and add ⅓ cup of water. Mix the flakes and water until they're a dough-like consistency. Add more soap flakes or water as needed. Then have kids scoop out a spoonful of soapy dough and form the dough into small soap balls around the center of the twine. Tie the ends of the twine in a small knot.

As kids work, have them tell about ways to demonstrate their love to others, such as kind acts, helping with chores, giving warm hugs, speaking kindly, and praying for others.

When the soap balls are finished, place them on the foil to dry. Say: **What neat soap balls. You know, they are good reminders of how Jesus served his disciples by washing their feet. Let's review all the disciple truths as you hold up each item in your Disciple Kit.**

Truth 1: A disciple has faith in God's promises. (PVC pipe)

Truth 2: A disciple celebrates Jesus. (party horn)

Truth 3: A disciple learns about God. (phylactery box)

Truth 4: A disciple trusts Jesus. (boat-in-a-bottle)

Truth 5: A disciple seeks Jesus. (sunglasses)

Truth 6: A disciple serves Jesus and others. (spoon person)

Truth 7: A disciple build his life on Jesus. (cornerstone)

Truth 8: A disciple helps others stay close to God. (coin rubbings)

Truth 9: A disciple obeys God. (sign)

Truth 10: A disciple loves others. (soap ball)

Say: **Wow! What a great list of important things for a disciple to remember and put into action! We only have a few more items to add, then we'll be done with our kits—but not with learning how to be powerful disciples for Jesus! That's a lifelong thing! We've been learning about how Jesus demonstrated his love for us; now let's demonstrate our love for God's Word!** When the soap balls are dry, wrap them in foil and place them in the Disciple Kits.

SUPER SCRIPTURE

Before class, draw the John 3:16 rebus puzzle by enlarging and photocopying the patterns on page 126. You'll also need to make a copy of the patterns for each child. Color and cut out your enlarged rebus puzzle pieces and assemble them on poster

board with words to make the rebus Scripture verse in the margin. Tape the puzzle to the wall or a door for kids to see. You'll use this puzzle for the next few weeks, so keep it handy! To save time during class, cut large sheets of poster board into fourths so children can make their own rebus Scripture verses to take home. Use one large sheet for every four kids.

Gather kids in front of the rebus Scripture verse. Invite kids to "read" the verse using the words and pictures. Then read the verse as you point to the pictures and words. Say: **This is probably one of the best loved, most well-known verses from the Bible because it tells us just how much God loves us! God loves us so much that he sent his only Son, Jesus, to us. And whoever believes in Jesus will have everlasting life in heaven. That's a very powerful verse, isn't it?** Ask:

★ **How was sending Jesus a great way for God to show his love for us?**

★ **Why is it important to believe in and love Jesus?**

★ **What promise does God make to those who believe in Jesus?**

Say: **I want to help you learn this verse, and using the rebus puzzle is a great way to do that. It's also fun! Who can read the verse once more for us using the rebus puzzle?**

When a volunteer has read the verse, hand each child a copy of the rebus patterns and a piece of poster board. Let kids work in small groups or pairs to color and cut out the patterns. Have kids glue the pictures to their pieces of poster board and add the words to the verse.

When the posters are done, have kids take turns reading the verse in their small groups. Then say: **Take your posters home and hang them where you can practice this very important verse each day! Why, you may even be able to help some of your family members or friends learn John 3:16 with your rebus Scripture puzzle! That would be a wonderful demonstration of your love for them and for God! Remember, disciples love others and God, too! Now let's demonstrate our love for the Lord and for each other by offering a special prayer and promise.**

A POWERFUL PROMISE

You'll need the Find a Coin bank from lesson 8.

Have kids sit in a circle and ask for a moment of silence, then say: **We've learned today that Jesus demonstrated his love for us in many ways, by serving, teaching, sharing, and praying. We've discovered that disciples love others and Jesus, too, and are happy to demonstrate their love in** many ways, just as Jesus did. And we've worked on the Mighty Memory Verse that tells us how much the Lord loves us. John 3:16 says (pause and encourage kids to repeat the verse with you), **"For God so loved the world that he gave his one and only Son, that whoever believes in him shall not perish but have eternal life."**

Hold up the Bible and say: **Jesus promised to share the bread and wine with us in heaven. And he also promised to love and help us forever.** Read aloud John 13:35 again. Then continue: **Let's demonstrate our love as disciples by promising to carry on his example of loving others. We'll pass the Bible, and you can say, "I will show my love to someone each day this week, Lord."** Pass the Bible until everyone has had a chance to make a promise. Close with a prayer thanking Jesus for showing us his love and for showing us how to express our own love to others. End with a corporate "amen." If children brought coins for the Find a Coin bank, have them donate their offerings at this time.

Say: **Being a disciple is so exciting! I'm thankful we're disciples of Jesus and learning to be even better followers of his! Let's show how happy we are to be Jesus' disciples by repeating the disciple rap we learned a few weeks ago!**

I'm not just a follower—that couldn't be much hollower!
I'm not just a sin-quitter, quiet Christian, pew-sitter!
I'M A DISCIPLE! A DISCIPLE OF JESUS!

I learn the lessons Jesus taught;
I know my life by him was bought;
Jesus is my every thought—
I'M A DISCIPLE! A DISCIPLE OF JESUS!

I trust in help that Jesus brings;
He's in control of everything;
I'll praise his name and shout and sing—
I'M A DISCIPLE! A DISCIPLE OF JESUS!

End with this responsive good-bye:
Leader: **May you show others your love.**
Children: **And also you!**

Distribute the Power Page! take-home papers as kids are leaving and remind them to take home their rebus Scripture puzzles to practice. Thank children for coming and encourage them to keep their promises this week.

POWER PAGE!

Special Supper

Use Matthew 26:26-28 to fill in the missing words, then supply the letters to find the name of the special meal Jesus shared with his disciples.

"While they were eating, __ __ __ __
<u>   1   3 </u>

took __ __ __ __ __, gave __ __ __ __ __ __
<u> 4   9 </u>   <u>2 6</u>

and broke it, ... saying, 'Take and eat; this is my body.' Then he took the __ __ __ ,
<u>   5 </u>

gave thanks and offered it, saying, '... This

is my __ __ __ __ of the covenant, which
<u> 8 7 </u>

is poured out for many for the forgiveness of __ __ __ __ .'"
<u>10</u>

__ __ __ __ __ __ __ __ , __ __ __ __ __ __
2 6 1 8 7 4 9 10   10 3 5 5 1 4

REMEMBER-ME SANDWICHES

Jesus offered bread and wine at the Last Supper so we'd remember that he gave his life to forgive our sins. Make these simple sandwiches to share with your family's supper—and remember what Jesus did for us.

Use a ♥-shaped cookie cutter to cut slices of bread into hearts and remind you of Jesus' unending love. Spread each heart with grape jelly (wine is made from grapes). Now you have bread and "wine" jelly spread over hearts of love! Before you enjoy your treats, offer a prayer of thanks for all Jesus has given us.

Memory Match-Up

Draw matching lines from the blanks to the pictures that represent the missing words to John 3:16.

_____ _____ _____ _____ _____

the _____ that he _____

his _____ and only _____ , that

whoever _____ in him

shall _____ perish but _____

eternal life. John 3:16

Disciples have
a spirit of
thankfulness.

Matthew 26–28
Romans 5:6-8

SESSION SUPPLIES

★ Bibles

★ scissors and markers

★ two paper sacks and pins

★ blue and white construction
paper

★ shiny wrapping paper or
aluminum foil

★ crepe paper and a stapler or
tape

★ tempera paints and brushes

★ white copy paper

★ photocopies of the Would
You cards (page 126)

★ photocopies of the Power
Page! (page 105)

THANK YOU, JESUS!

MIGHTY MEMORY VERSE

For God so loved the world that he gave his one and
only Son, that whoever believes in him shall not perish but
have eternal life. John 3:16
*(For older kids, add in John 13:34a: "A new command I
give you: Love one another.")*

SESSION OBJECTIVES

During this session, children will
★ realize that Jesus died for us because he loved us
★ understand that Jesus obeyed God's will
★ learn that disciples have an attitude of gratitude
★ thank Jesus for his sacrifice of love

BIBLE BACKGROUND

"Thank you for shopping at our store." "Thanks for the
ride." "Thank you, and have a nice day!" How many times
a day or week do we repeat or hear words of rote thanks?
We master rote repetition of thanks from a young age when
we're taught that we should say the words but never *what*
they truly mean or *why* we're to feel them. How then do
we find the sincerest, most personal way to thank Jesus for
all he's given and done for us? By relearning what thanks
truly means and by realizing that words alone are insuffi-
cient! Thanks needs to come from deep in our hearts and
souls and be expressed through word, deeds, and a general
attitude of gratitude!

For years kids have heard, "What do you say?" and "Remember your manners; say thank you!" It's no wonder that thanks soon becomes an unthinking and often unfeeling habit. Use this lesson to let kids explore personal ways of expressing their thanks to Jesus for his love and sacrifice on the cross and to encourage kids to turn two little over-used, under-felt words into a lifetime of thanksgiving and praise!

POWER FOCUS

Before class, cut out the Would You cards from page 126. Be sure you have one People and one Thing card for each child plus one set of Jesus cards. Cut the cards apart, then place the People cards in one paper sack and the Things cards in another. Label the sacks. Hold on to the two Jesus cards.

As kids arrive, greet them warmly and thank them for coming to class. Invite kids to sit in a circle and place the two paper sacks in the center of the circle. Say: **Let's start off with an unusual activity called Would You? Each person can go to the paper sacks and quickly choose one card from each. Then return to your place and silently read your cards, but keep them secret!**

As soon as everyone has a card from each sack, say: **Silently read the Thing card you have and ask yourself, "Would I give up this thing for the person on my other card?" Think carefully and honestly about what your answer would be!** Allow a few moments for kids to reflect, then say: **You might have a very hard decision! It's not always easy to give up things we know or love, is it? And it's especially difficult if we have to give up something precious for someone we don't even know! Would anyone like to share what's on your cards and tell us what you would do and why?**

Allow volunteers to share if they wish. When everyone who would like a turn has had one, ask:

★ **What helped you decide whether or not to give up your thing for the person on your card?**

★ **If someone gave up something precious for you, how would you feel? How could you say thank you?**

Say: **It's just human to have a hard time making decisions like these, isn't it? I'm glad we're not called on to do that very often! But someone was called on to give up something very valuable. Let me read the two cards I have, and you see if you can guess whose cards they could have been.** Read aloud the two Jesus cards, then say: **This person gave up his life for all the people in the world. Who do you think he was?**

Allow kids time to share their thoughts and encourage them to explain why they think it may be Jesus. Then say: **Yes, these could have been Jesus' cards. Jesus gave up his life for all the people in the world—for people who hadn't even been born yet! And Jesus gave up his life with love for each of us. Wow! Now that deserves a special thank-you right from the heart, doesn't it? Today, we'll discover why Jesus had to die and what his death means for us. We'll also learn that Jesus' death was yet another way he gave his love to us and that we can thank him in special ways. We'll also review our powerful Mighty Memory Verse that tells how much God loves us. Right now, let's learn more about the great sacrifice Jesus made and why.**

THE MIGHTY MESSAGE

Before class, cut out two blue construction-paper tear drops for each child. Then cover a bulletin board or area on the wall with shiny wrapping paper or aluminum foil. Add the words "Sad Tears to Glad Tears!" at the top of the display. For a finishing touch, attach twisted blue and white or purple and white crepe paper around the edges.

Seat kids in front of the shiny background and set pins nearby. Hand each child two paper tear drops and a marker. Ask someone to read the title of the display, then say: **This is the sad and glad story of Jesus' love for us. We'll use these paper tear drops to retell the story of Jesus' sad death and glad resurrection! When you hear a sad part in the story, hold up one tear drop—a sad tear—and make a thumbs-down signal. But when you hear a happy part, hold up the other tear—a tear of joy—and smile and give a thumbs up!**

Then quietly retell the story of Jesus' death and resurrection from Matthew 26–28: **Jesus had come to love us. He had been sent by our heavenly Father to heal, help, teach, and love us all.** Pause for kids to respond with happy signals. Then continue: **But many people didn't love Jesus, and they didn't believe he was God's Son.** Pause for kids to respond with sad signals, then continue: **The people who didn't have faith in or love Jesus decided that Jesus should die.** Pause for responses. **Think of** how Jesus must have felt. He had loved everyone and had given them God's truth. Jesus had helped and healed people. Jesus had forgiven people, accepted even the most unlovable people, and had treated everyone with love. Yet here he was—dying for them. Pause for kids to respond with their tear drops and sad signals.

Say: **Why did Jesus have to die? Jesus willingly died to fulfill God's plan for our forgiveness and salvation. Jesus died to make our sins right with God so we could be close to God and live with him in heaven. Jesus died for us because he loved us!** Wait for kids to respond with glad tears and thumbs-up signals.

After Jesus' death on the cross, he was buried in a tomb; a big stone sealed it closed. Pause for kids to make sad signals. **His disciples were very sad because they missed Jesus and his perfect love.** Pause. **But on the third day after Jesus died, some of his friends went to his tomb, and what did they see? An angel who told them that Jesus was alive!** Wait for kids to respond with glad signals. **Jesus had risen and was no longer dead—just as God's plan promised! And Jesus is alive today and still here helping, healing, teaching, and loving us!** Have kids respond a last time with the thumbs-up happy signal. Then ask:

★ **What did Jesus' death do for us?**

★ **In what ways did Jesus demonstrate his love for us?**

★ **How can we express our thanks to Jesus for his sacrifice of love?**

Say: **Jesus gave his life so we could be forgiven and have eternal life. As a thank-you to Jesus, let's begin to finish our display. Write something you can thank Jesus for on one of your tear drops, and we'll turn the sad tears to glad tears!** Suggest thank-yous such as "Thank you for loving me," "Thank you for giving your life so I can live forever," and "Thank you for teaching me how to love."

When the thank-yous are done, have kids pin them to the display. Then say: **Hold on to your other tear drop—we'll add it to our display later. But first, let's put another item in our Disciple Kits.**

THE MESSAGE IN **MOTION**

Before class cut sheets of white construction paper in half down the center, a half sheet for each child. You will also need a stack of white copy paper, colorful tempera paints, and brushes or cotton swabs. Also, you'll want to prepare a sample card by following the directions below.

Set the paints, brushes, and white construction paper on the table. Hold up the card you made and say: **Isn't this a beautiful thank-you card? I painted the front in a lovely swirl design and inside I've written a short thank-you to Jesus! Let me read it to you.**

Read aloud the inside of your card and show kids how you decorated it. Then say: **You can make your own neat thank-you card to Jesus with your own swirly design. Everyone's card will look unique because everyone has his or her own way of thanking the Lord!**

Show kids how to fold a sheet of copy paper in half, then in half again. Open up the paper and use a paintbrush or cotton swab to put a drop or blob of three paint colors in the center of the paper side by side. (Don't use too much paint or put the paint drops on top of one another!) Then gently refold the paper. Softly rub the folds to spread the paint a bit, then carefully open up the paper and look at the great design. Finally, fold a piece of white construction paper in half, then lay the front of your soon-to-be-card on the paint design. Again, gently rub or press on the design to transfer it to the card. Lift the card from the paper and you have a lovely design on the front!

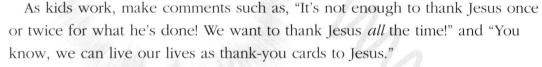

Have kids blow on their designs for several minutes to dry them, then open the cards and write thank-yous to Jesus. Finally, have kids decorate the insides of their cards with hearts, flowers, stars, crosses, or whatever designs they'd like.

As kids work, make comments such as, "It's not enough to thank Jesus once or twice for what he's done! We want to thank Jesus *all* the time!" and "You know, we can live our lives as thank-you cards to Jesus."

When the cards are complete, tell kids they'll read their thank-you cards a little later. Then have kids hold their Disciple Kits as you say: **The cards you made are beautiful, and they are the eleventh item for your Disciple Kits! Let's review all the truths together as you hold up each item.**

Truth 1: A disciple has faith in God's promises. (PVC pipe)
Truth 2: A disciple celebrates Jesus. (party horn)
Truth 3: A disciple learns about God. (phylactery box)
Truth 4: A disciple trusts Jesus. (boat-in-a-bottle)
Truth 5: A disciple seeks Jesus. (sunglasses)
Truth 6: A disciple serves Jesus and others. (spoon person)

Truth 7: A disciple build his life on Jesus. (cornerstone)

Truth 8: A disciple helps others stay close to God. (coin rubbings)

Truth 9: A disciple obeys God. (sign)

Truth 10: A disciple loves others. (soap ball)

Truth 11: A disciple thanks Jesus. (thank-you card)

Say: **These are important truths to remember, and knowing them will help us become powerful, thankful disciples our whole lives through! Now let's show that proud disciples love learning God's Word, just as truth number three taught us!**

Set the thank-you cards aside to read during the Powerful Promise.

SUPER SCRIPTURE

Be sure the Scripture rebus puzzle from last week is on the wall or door for kids to see. Gather kids in front of the puzzle and invite several pairs of volunteers to use the words and pictures to read the verse. Have one partner repeat the verse as the other partner points to the words and pictures. Then repeat the verse in unison three times.

Say: **This is the all-important verse that tells us how much God loves us! He loved us enough to send his only Son, Jesus, to love and forgive us and to offer us a way to live forever in heaven.** Read Romans 5:6-8, then ask:

★ **What might have happened if God's love wasn't so big and perfect?**

★ **How can we express our thanks to God and to Jesus for their love?**

Say: **You know, saying thank you is important, but sometimes we say those two little words without really thinking about what they mean or taking time to truly think about what we're giving thanks for! The words become stale and too easy to blurt out without meaning. We want to be sure that the Lord knows how thankful we are for his love and for Jesus' sacrifice on the cross for our sins. How can we do that?**

Allow kids to share their thoughts, then say: **We can thank the Lord not only through our words, but through our actions and the way we feel inside. In other words, we can have an attitude of gratitude!**

Let's write one way we can express our thanks to Jesus this week. It might be with a kind action, by helping someone with a chore or maybe through prayer or by promising to read the Bible each day. On your remaining tear drop, write the way you can show, not just tell, Jesus that you're thankful for his love. Have kids write on their tear drops, then pin them to the display you began earlier.

When all the tears of joy and thanksgiving are on display, read them aloud. Then say: **Now let's express our thanks in two more ways: through a promise and a prayer!** Keep the Scripture rebus puzzle on the wall for next week's lesson.

A POWERFUL PROMISE

You'll need the Find a Coin bank from lesson 8.

Have kids sit in a circle and hold the thank-you cards they made earlier. Quietly say: **What important things we've learned today! We've discovered that Jesus died to fulfill God's plan of salvation and forgiveness. We've learned that Jesus willingly died because he loved us and wanted us to live forever in heaven. And we've explored ways to have an attitude of gratitude that goes beyond just saying the words "thank you." Let's express our thankfulness by making a promise to show Jesus our thanks through the way we feel inside. It might be having a more loving, patient, or caring attitude or maybe giving Jesus more praise and honor. Perhaps it will be through prayer and reading the Bible. Whatever you choose, it will be your own expression of thanks.**

We'll pass the Bible, and as you hold it, silently make your promise to thank Jesus in some special way this week. Pass the Bible until everyone has had a turn to make a promise. Then say: **Let's close by reading our thank-you cards as a prayer to Jesus. We'll take turns reading the cards, then end with "amen."**

Continue reading the thank-you cards until everyone has had a turn sharing. Then end with a corporate "amen." If kids brought coins for the Find a Coin bank, have them donate their offerings at this time. Then say: **As you go through today, tomorrow, and each day this week, remember that disciples thank Jesus with an attitude of gratitude in all they do and say!**

Have kids place their thank-you cards in their Disciple Kits, then end by repeating John 3:16. Close with this responsive good-bye:

Leader: **May you live a thankful life for Jesus.**

Children: **And also you!**

Distribute the Power Page! take-home papers as kids are leaving. Thank children for coming and encourage them to keep their promises this week.

POWER PAGE!

QUIZ CODE!

Why did Jesus have to die? Use the code to find 4 reasons Jesus died for us.

1. __ __ __ __ __ __ __ __ __ __ __
   ■ ◆ ✳ ◆ ● ✖ ☆ ♥ ✓ ✝ ★

2. __ __ __ __ __ __ __ __ __
   ■ ◆ ◆ ✡ ✓ ➤ ✖ ◆ ♣

3. __ __ __ __ __ __ __ __ __ __ __ __
   ■ ◆ ★ ✧ ◆ ✺ ✝ ★ ❑ ◆ ♥ ✓

4. __ __ __ __ __ __ __ __ __ __ __ __ __
   ■ ◆ ✖ ☆ ♥ ✓ ✝ ★ ❑ ☆ ✳ ✓

B	D	E	F	G	H	I	L
✡	♣	✓	✳	✖	✧	☆	❑

O	R	S	T	U	V	W	Y
◆	●	★	■	✝	♥	✺	➤

Easter Treats

Share the celebration of Jesus' life by sharing these cool eggs with friends!

You'll need:
★ plastic, pull-apart eggs
★ colored paper and pens
★ a paint brush or cotton swabs
★ craft glue   ★ confetti

Directions:
1. Spread glue on the egg halves and roll them in confetti.
2. While the egg halves dry, copy John 3:16 or the words "He has risen!" on paper strips.
3. Place a strip in each egg, then give the eggs to your friends.

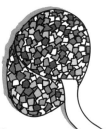

Find the missing words to John 3:16 and cross them out in the puzzle. Then write the words on the correct blanks below.

For ____ **so** _____ **the** _____ **that**

he _____ **his** ____ **and** _____ ____ **, that**

_____ _____ **in him** _____ **not**

_____ **but** _____ **eternal** ____ .

John 3:16

Y	P	S	O	N	X	W
K	W	O	R	L	D	N
Z	S	G	Z	O	B	X
W	H	O	E	V	E	R
B	A	D	J	E	L	H
O	L	K	Z	D	I	A
N	L	L	O	N	E	V
L	M	I	G	A	V	E
Y	B	F	J	X	E	W
A	P	E	R	I	S	H

SHOW 'EM THE WAY!

Disciples lead others to Jesus.

Matthew 28:16-20
John 13:34, 35; 21:15-17

SESSION SUPPLIES

★ Bibles
★ a bell to ring
★ scissors and markers
★ wallpaper sample books
★ paper and glue or tape
★ photocopies of the lamb pattern (page 112)
★ photocopies of John 3:16 (page 127) and the rhyming card (page 110)
★ photocopies of the Whiz Quiz (page 114) and the Power Page! (page 113)

MIGHTY MEMORY VERSE

For God so loved the world that he gave his one and only Son, that whoever believes in him shall not perish but have eternal life. John 3:16

(For older kids, add in John 13:34a: "A new command I give you: Love one another.")

SESSION OBJECTIVES

During this session, children will
★ discover that Jesus wants us tell others about him
★ learn that disciples lead others to Jesus
★ explore ways to witness about the Lord
★ understand the importance of sharing Jesus with others

BIBLE BACKGROUND

Which is easier: witnessing to someone or leading someone to Jesus and then discipling him or her? It's generally easier just to quickly tell someone about the wonders of Jesus and the difference he's made in our lives than to lead someone step by step to Jesus. But in John 21, Jesus commanded Peter to "feed my lambs" and "take care of my sheep." Leading and feeding both require more than just telling—they require time, patience, action, and accountability. A good shepherd would never just toss a lamb a crumb, then leave it to fend for itself! And as Jesus' loving disciples and ambassadors, we want to shepherd his people through caring actions, encouraging words, God's truths, and Christ's love. Be challenged to find a lamb for Jesus, then feed and lead that lamb home to the good shepherd who leads us all—Jesus!

Kids are usually the followers. They march behind teachers to recess, they walk behind parents at the store, and they tend to think that adults, being older, are the only ones who can be leaders. Help kids realize they can be powerful disciples who lead for Jesus! Use this lesson to introduce kids to witnessing for Christ, then leading people to really know and love the Lord.

POWER focus

Before class choose a bell that is easy to ring and place it on a chair at one end of the room.

As kids arrive greet them warmly and have them form pairs. Have everyone stand at the opposite end of the room from the bell. Explain that in this game one partner will close her eyes while the other partner leads her to the bell, which is then to be rung. When the bell is rung, switch places so the leader becomes the follower and return to the starting place. Encourage kids to be creative in the ways they choose to lead their partners. Holding hands may be one way, guiding with hands on shoulders may be another way, or having nonseeing partners hold on to collars or elbows might be other ways.

When everyone has returned to the starting place, ask:

★ **What was it like to be the leader? What responsibilities did you feel?**

★ **How did you feel being led by your partner?**

★ **In what ways did trust play a role in leading and being led?**

★ **How is this like leading someone to Jesus?**

Say: **Leading people isn't always easy, and we have to trust that we can find ways to help them! That's how it is when we lead others to Jesus and help others discover Jesus' love and forgiveness. And just as there were many ways to lead our partners in the game, there are many ways disciples can lead others to Jesus!**

Today we'll discover why it's important to share Jesus with other people. We'll learn what kinds of things to tell others about Jesus and how we can effectively lead them to know, love, and follow the Lord. And we'll also review our Mighty Memory Verse that teaches how much God loves us.

Right now, let's discover how the disciples learned that Jesus wants us to lead others to him!

THE MIGHTY MESSAGE

Before class enlarge and photocopy on stiff paper the lamb pattern on page 112. Make a copy for each child. To save class time, cut out the patterns, especially if you have young kids.

Hand each child a marker and a lamb pattern, then have kids form small groups. Say: **In the Bible, Jesus tells us that he is the good shepherd and that we are his sheep. Jesus wants us to know that he cares for us, leads us, and feeds us with God's truths and that we are sheep who follow and love him. These paper sheep remind us of being Jesus' lambs, and we'll use the lambs during our Bible message. When you hear the word *lamb* or *sheep*, pop up and say, "I love my shepherd, Jesus!"**

Read aloud John 21:15-17 and pause each time you read the word *lamb* or *sheep* and wait for kids to respond. Then say: **Wow! Jesus asked something of Peter three times. What did Jesus ask Peter so many times?** Encourage kids to tell that Jesus asked Peter if he loved him. Then ask: **What was Peter's reply each time?**

Say: **Three times Jesus asked if Peter loved him, and each time Peter told Jesus that he did love him. And each time, Jesus told Peter to do something.** Ask:

★ **What did Jesus ask Peter to do?**

★ **Who do you think Jesus meant by "my sheep"?** (Help kids understand that, just as in the passage about the good shepherd, Jesus referred to people as his sheep.)

★ **Why do you think Jesus wanted Peter to care for people?**

Say: **Jesus wanted Peter to feed his people on God's Word and to teach them God's truths and the true way to heaven, through Jesus. Jesus also wanted Peter to care for his people and lead them to him. In other words, Jesus wanted Peter to lead and feed his people! Let's write the words *lead* and *feed* on our sheep.**

Have kids write the word *lead* at the top of their sheep and the word *feed* in the middle. Then say: **Jesus wanted his disciple Peter to lead and feed his people, and he wants all of his disciples to do the same!** Ask:

★ **How can we lead people to Jesus?** (Have kids suggest ways such as telling others about Jesus, prayer, kindness, love, and modeling Jesus' behavior. Then help kids write two or three of those ways on their sheep under the word *lead.*)

★ **How can we feed people, that is, tell them about Jesus?** (Have kids suggest ways such as telling them that Jesus died for them, that Jesus forgives us, that we can live with God forever, and that Jesus loves them. Then help kids write two or three of those truths on their sheep under the word *feed.*)

Say: **Jesus wants everyone to know, love, and follow him. And as his disciples, we can lead others to Jesus! Why is it important for others to know Jesus?** Allow several minutes for kids to tell their thoughts, then say: **Disciples lead others to Jesus because they love other people and because they love the Lord! Let's add our last item to the Disciple Kits to remind us to lead others to Jesus and to tell them how wonderful he is!**

THE MESSAGE IN **MOTION**

Before class, collect several old wallpaper sample books from home center or decorating stores. The books are usually free for the asking! You'll also need to photocopy the Scripture strip for John 3:16 from page 127 and the rhyming card on page 110, one of each for each child.

Have kids form small groups and hand each group a wallpaper sample book, glue or tape, and markers. Give each child a Scripture strip and a small rhyming card. Explain that kids will be creating tracts. Tell kids that a tract is something Christians give to others to explain who Jesus is and why it's so wonderful to have Jesus in our lives.

Have kids choose pages from the wallpaper book and cut them out. Fold over the page and glue or tape the card and John 3:16 inside, then decorate the front, back, and insides of the tracts.

When the tracts are finished, say: **Your tracts are great, and I challenge you to make even more of them at home to hand out to people. The more we share the truth about Jesus, the more people will know of his love! Wouldn't it be great if everyone in the whole world could know, love, and follow Jesus?**

Have kids open the Disciple Kits, then say: **Well! We've finished making our Disciple Kits, and just look how many wonderful treasures are inside! But do you remember all of the disciple's truths? Let's see!**

Truth 1: A disciple has faith in God's promises. (PVC pipe)

Truth 2: A disciple celebrates Jesus. (party horn)

Truth 3: A disciple learns about God. (phylactery box)

Truth 4: A disciple trusts Jesus. (boat-in-a-bottle)

Truth 5: A disciple seeks Jesus. (sunglasses)

Truth 6: A disciple serves Jesus and others. (spoon person)

Truth 7: A disciple build his life on Jesus. (cornerstone)

Truth 8: A disciple helps others stay close to God. (coin rubbings)

Truth 9: A disciple obeys God. (sign)

Truth 10: A disciple loves others. (soap ball)

Truth 11: A disciple thanks Jesus. (thank-you card)

Truth 12: A disciple leads others to Jesus. (tract)

Say: **Wow! That's a whole lot of truth, isn't it? At the end of today's lesson you can take your Disciple Kit home and share it with your family and friends. See if you can remember each truth as you show them the items in your kit and explain what being a disciple of Jesus is all about! Remember, a disciple leads and feeds others, and one of the best ways to do this is through God's Word. We have to know God's Word before we can lead others to it. Let's see how well you know the Mighty Memory Verse!**

> JESUS LOVES US, THAT'S FOR SURE—
> HIS LOVE IS WARM AND PERFECT-PURE!

SUPER SCRIPTURE

Before this activity, cut a sheet of paper into four pieces. Be sure you have the Scripture rebus puzzle from last week on the wall or door.

Gather kids in front of the puzzle and hand a piece of paper to each of four kids. Have the kids hold their papers over different pictures or words in the verse, then call on a volunteer to repeat the verse. If she gets it right, give a lively round of applause and choose four more kids to do the great "cover up." Continue until everyone has had a turn to cover a portion of the puzzle and repeat the verse.

Say: **I just love this verse because it tells us so powerfully how much God loves us all. You know, if everyone who doesn't know the Lord could hear this verse, I think they would want to come home to the Lord with glad hearts, don't you? And as disciples, you can spread this verse to others! If you still have your Scripture rebus posters from a few weeks ago, give the poster to someone you would like to lead to Jesus to hang on the wall and learn. You can also present your tract to someone to tell that person of Jesus' love.** Ask:

★ **How can knowing Jesus help others?**

★ **What can you tell someone about Jesus?**

★ **Who can you tell about Jesus this week? next week?**

Say: **God sent Jesus to love us, and Jesus wants us to spread his love to others. So let's share a prayer and ask for the Lord's help in leading others to Jesus.**

A POWERFUL PROMISE

You'll need the Find a Coin bank from lesson 8.

Have kids sit in a circle and ask for a moment of silence, then say: **We've learned today that Jesus wants us to lead and feed his people and that disciples can lead others to Jesus. We've explored ways to lead others to Christ and learned what we can tell others about Jesus. We've also worked on the Mighty Memory Verse that reminds us how great God's love for us is. John 3:16 says** (pause and encourage kids to repeat the verse with you), **"For God so loved the world that he gave his one and only Son, that whoever believes in him shall not perish but have eternal life."** If you have older kids, also repeat the extra challenge verse.

Read aloud Matthew 28:16-20 and John 13:34, 35. Say: **Jesus wanted Peter, the other disciples, and his disciples today to lead and feed his people in love and with willing hearts. Let's make a special promise to be disciples who obey Jesus and witness to others about him as we lead them with love to the Lord! As we pass the Bible around the circle, say, "I'll**

lead and feed your people, Lord." Pass the Bible until everyone has had a chance to make a promise. End with a prayer asking Jesus' help in bringing others to him. End with a corporate "amen." If kids brought coins for the Find a Coin bank, have them donate their gifts at this time.

Before kids leave, allow five or ten minutes to complete the Whiz Quiz from page 114. If you run out of time, be sure to do this page first thing next week.

If there's time, sing the disciple's marching song from page 60. Then end with this responsive good-bye:

Leader: **May you lead others to Jesus.**

Children: **And also you!**

Distribute the Power Page! take-home papers as kids are leaving and remind them to take home their Disciple Kits. Thank children for coming and encourage them to keep their promises this week.

POWER PAGE!

SPREAD the NEWS!

Name 2 people in your family who you can tell about Jesus.

_____ _____

Name 2 friends you can tell about Jesus.

_____ _____

List 3 things you can tell about Jesus!

1. _____

2. _____

3. _____

Sheep Truffles

Make a fold of sweet sheep to remind your family how we're to LEAD and FEED others for Jesus!

Mix 1 box of powdered sugar with ½ teaspoon softened butter and 2 teaspoons milk to make a pliable dough. (Add milk if dough is stiff.)

Roll spoonfuls of candy dough into balls, then quickly dip the balls in milk and roll them in flaked coconut. Nibble your treats as you read Luke 15:3-7.

Fill in the missing high, low, and in-between letters to complete John 3:16.

High & LOW

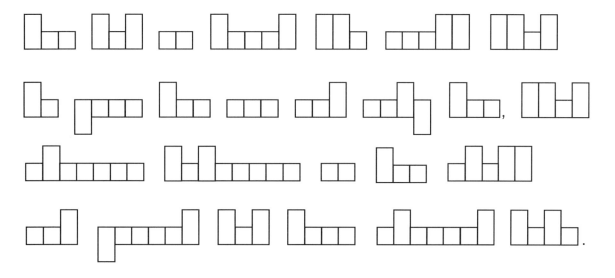

WHIZ QUIZ

Color in T (true) or F (false) to answer the following questions.

1. Jesus served his disciples.   (T) (F)

2. The bread and wine are called the Lord's Breakfast.   (T) (F)

3. Jesus is the only way to God and forgiveness.   (T) (F)

4. Jesus' death was not a part of God's plan of salvation.   (T) (F)

5. We don't need to tell others about Jesus.   (T) (F)

6. Jesus died for us because he loved us.   (T) (F)

7. Disciples don't need to thank Jesus.   (T) (F)

Scripture Swirl

Unscramble the words below, then fill them in to complete the **MIGHTY MEMORY VERSE.**

elvod loved
wrlod world
yonl only
nSo Son
Gdo God
vage gave
ohwevre whoever
mhi him
sherpi shepir
naterel
elif life

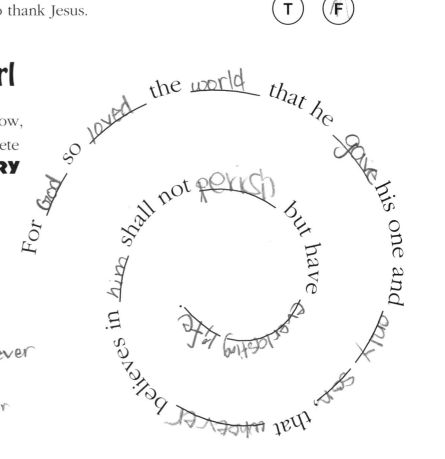

For God so loved the world that he gave his one and only Son, that whoever believes in him shall not perish but have everlasting life.

REVIEW
LESSON

By this all men will know
that you are my disciples,
if you love one another.
John 13:35

DISCIPLE MAKERS

Disciples are proud to know, love, and follow Jesus!

Philippians 3:10
2 Corinthians 10:17

SESSION SUPPLIES

★ Bibles
★ white nylon fabric
★ red and yellow craft felt
★ black vinyl letters
★ tacky craft glue and scissors
★ dowel rods
★ gold braid trim
★ paper and markers
★ photocopies of all the Scripture strips (page 127)

MIGHTY MEMORY VERSE

This is a review lesson of all four previous verses: 1 John 4:14; Philippians 2:10, 11; John 14:6; and John 3:16.

SESSION OBJECTIVES

During this session, children will
★ review what a disciple is and does
★ discover that disciples spend their lives serving Jesus
★ realize that we can take pride in being Jesus' disciples
★ express their joy in being Jesus' disciples

BIBLE BACKGROUND

It seems that everything has a natural ending. Movies come to a close, roads finally stop or turn off, and curtains come down on plays. But there's one thing that never stops, one job that's never done: being a disciple of Jesus! By the mere definition of a disciple, we go on learning and continuing to grow in knowledge, in spirit, and in the ways we serve the Lord. Discipleship is a continuation not only of time and effort but of Jesus' perfect love! Jesus trusts us as disciples to continue the love, acceptance, and teaching he began so many years ago and guides us in today. There's nothing so stirring, so exciting, and so challenging as being a disciple. The hours may be long and filled, but the rewards are heavenly!

Kids have a tendency to forget things if they're out of mind or sight. That's why it's important to instill a sense of belonging, pride, and responsibility in being disciples and to help kids see that their roles as Jesus' ambassadors and torch-bearers is important and wonderful enough to last forever! Use this lively review lesson to inspire "disciple pride" in your kids and to help them celebrate the best job they'll ever love!

POWER FOCUS

Before class, purchase several yards of white nylon fabric. Kids will be making awesome flags that really fly and wave in the wind (see page 122), and nylon fabric will make the flags look realistic. Don't be afraid to spend a little bit more; remember that this lesson should be very memorable as it wraps up the entire book! You'll also need red and yellow craft felt, gold braid trim, a 3-foot by ½-inch dowel rod for each child, and several packages of vinyl stick-on letters.

For this activity, you'll need to cut the white nylon fabric into rectangles that are 24-by-18-inches, one for each child. Lightly draw two straight lines across the center of the flag and about four inches apart. Kids will use them as guidelines for attaching their stick-on letters. You'll also need to either sew or glue a rod pocket along one side of each flag for the dowel rod to be slipped into later.

As kids arrive, greet them by saying, "**Hello, disciples! I'm so glad you're here!**" Hand each child a white nylon rectangle and say: **Wave your flags to show you're proud to be a disciple! Yeah!**

Lead kids in a march around the room as you sing the disciple's marching song to the tune of "The Ants Go Marching One-By-One." Have kids wave the flags as they march.

Oh, I'm a disciple of the Lord, hurrah! (XX), *hurrah!* (XX)
Oh, I'm a disciple of the Lord, hurrah! (XX), *hurrah!* (XX)
J-E-S-U-S is his name.
His power and glory I'll always proclaim.
I'm a d-i-s-c-i (XX) *p-l-e* (XX) *that's all I* (XX) *want to be!*
Boom, boom, boom, boom! Boom, boom, boom ... (repeat the song)

Say: **Wow! That was great but not as great as being a disciple of Jesus! That's the best thing anyone could be! Why are you glad and proud to be Jesus' disciple?** Invite kids to share their feelings about being disciples, then continue: **We've spent several weeks learning about being disciples. And** the first thing we learned was that a disciple is someone who learns from and follows the Master. But there's much more to being a disciple, so today we'll be reviewing what a disciple does, how a disciple serves Jesus and others, and what truths a disciple must know. And all the while we'll be assembling really cool flags to show our pride in being Jesus' disciples.

You have the beginning part of your fabulous flags, but they'll become more and more complete—just as we become more and more complete disciples who follow Jesus. Let's sing our song once more, then sit in the center of the room so we can review the exciting Bible stories we've learned.

Have kids march around the room once more singing the marching song, then sit on the floor.

POWER POINTERS

Let kids stand in two rows as people are leaving the church and hold their flags high for the entire congregation to pass through.

THE **MIGHTY** MESSAGE

Before this activity, make sure you have enough vinyl stick-on letters for kids to use on their flags. For each flag, you'll need the following letters: two each of the letters P, D, and I; and one each of the letters S, C, L, E, R, O, and U. Set the letters beside you during the activity, arranging them in piles of like letters.

Have kids form small groups. Say: **It's important to review what we've learned so we don't forget it. And right now we're going to review the Bible stories and passages we've learned during the past few weeks. Let's make our review into a fun game in which you can earn letters to go on your flags. I'll ask a question, and when your group knows the answer, wave your flags. You can give your answer, and if the other groups agree, they'll wave their flags. If you give the right answer, everyone waving a flag gets a letter. If a group disagrees with your answer and can tell the right answer, everyone in that group will get a letter. Ready?**

Ask the following questions and, when correct answers are given, distribute the letters one by one in order to spell out the word *disciple*.

★ **Since disciples are already smart, do they need to learn anything? Why or why not?** (Yes, disciples never stop learning about Jesus.)

★ **Did Jesus spend time learning about God and his truths?** (Yes, Jesus learned about God, and he also learned God's Word.)

★ **When disciples serve others, who else are they serving?** (Jesus)

★ **Who was the answer to God's greatest promise?** (Jesus)

★ **Why is it important to put Jesus first in our lives?** (So we focus on him; because he is our only leader; so we don't get into trouble)

★ **Can disciples obey just some of God's rules? Why or why not?** (No, we must obey all God's rules, just as Jesus did.)

★ **How did Jesus teach us to serve others?** (By serving his disciples; by washing the disciples' feet; by giving us the bread and wine.)

★ **Why did Jesus die for us?** (Because it fulfilled God's plan; because he loves us so much; so we could be forgiven.)

When everyone has a letter to the word *disciple*, ask kids if they know what their letters spell. Say: **Your letters spell out what you and I are—and are proud to be! They spell the word *disciple*. Let's add these letters to our flags.**

Show kids how to attach the letters to the word *disciple* across the top line that is drawn on their flags. Then say: **Well, look at your flags now! They're beginning to take shape. Are you ready to work for the next piece of your disciple flags? Then let's get started!**

THE MESSAGE IN MOTION

Before class, write the word *proud* on a sheet of paper and tape it to the wall or door for kids to see.

Invite kids to form pairs or trios and hand each group a sheet of paper and a marker. Then say: **This time we're going to play a word game to review what it means to be disciples. As disciples, we're proud to serve Jesus and to follow him in everything we say and do. So we'll spell the word *proud*. I'll give you several minutes to think of words that begin with each letter in the word *proud*. These words must describe what a disciple does or how a disciple serves Jesus. For example, for the letter u you may choose the word *understand*, which means we seek to understand more about God. Or maybe you'd choose the word *under* to remember that there is no other name under heaven by which we must be saved. When we're finished, we'll read our lists and you'll receive the letters to the word *proud*!**

Allow about five minutes for kids to think up words that describe disciples or how they serve Jesus. Give hints and helps as needed as you circulate from group to group.

Call time and invite each group to read the words they came up with. When each group has had a turn, give everyone a lively round of applause and pass out the letters to the word *proud*. Instruct kids to attach the letters on the line under the word *disciple*, centered under that word.

Say: **What do your flags say now? I think you're disciple proud!** Read aloud Philippians 3:10a and 2 Corinthians 10:17, then ask:

★ **When do you think it's okay to be proud? to boast?**

★ **What does it mean to be disciple proud?**

★ **Why is it great to feel pride and goodness in being Jesus' disciples?**

★ **How does being proud to be a disciple affect the way we serve Jesus? serve others? view ourselves?**

Say: **There are many Christians around the world, but it's sad to say that many aren't active disciples! They're happy just to sit in church and not put their faith into action for the Lord. I'm so glad we've learned so much about being disciples and about how to put our faith and love into action serving Jesus and others.**

Now let's review the Mighty Memory Verses we've learned as we get ready to add the next pieces to our flags.

SUPER SCRIPTURE

Before class, make one photocopy of the Scripture strips (page 127) for the Mighty Memory Verses, one copy for every two kids. If you have older kids, include the extra challenge verses. Cut each strip into three pieces (two pieces if you have young children) and place the pieces in an envelope for each pair of kids. If you have young children, cut a red felt heart and a yellow cross from felt. If you have older kids, you may wish to let them cut out their own felt hearts and crosses.

Have kids form pairs and hand each pair an envelope. Say: **We've learned four Mighty Memory Verses during the past weeks. Before we play a** game, let's repeat each verse two times to refresh your memories. Repeat each of these verses twice: 1 John 4:14; Philippians 2:10, 11; John 14:6; and John 3:16.

Say: **Good for you! It's so important for disciples to learn God's Word. After all, Jesus learned God's Word and put it to use in his life every day! We can do the same when we know what God's Word says! In your envelopes, you have puzzle pieces for each Mighty Memory Verse we've learned. See if you and your partner can put each of the four verses together. When you're done, give each other high fives and shout, "Disciples love God's Word!"**

Circulate and give help as needed. When all the groups have completed the puzzles, say: **Nice job! Give each other a final high five for a job well done! You know, it takes patience, hard work, and a loving heart to learn God's Word. Let's add these hearts to your flags.**

Hand each child a red felt heart and have kids glue the hearts to the upper lefthand corners of their flags. Then say: **Jesus learned God's Word and put it to use in his life. Let's add a cross to remind us how Jesus set perfect examples we can follow as his disciples.** Hand each child a yellow felt cross and have kids glue the crosses to the lower righthand corners of their flags.

Say: **Hold up your flags and let me see how wonderful they look! We only have a few more items to add and your flags will be finished. Let's form a prayer circle and share a prayer as we finish the flags and thank Jesus for being someone we're proud to follow.**

A POWERFUL PROMISE

You'll need the Find a Coin bank from lesson 8.

Before class, ask permission to let your kids parade through the congregation waving their disciple flags and singing the disciple's marching song (page 117). It will be a treat for everyone!

Have kids sit in a circle and hold their disciple flags. Say: **We've spent many weeks learning the importance of being a disciple. We've discovered that disciples follow Jesus' examples of serving and loving others and of learning God's Word. We've learned that disciples obey God and trust his promises. And we've explored ways to express our thanks and praise to Jesus for his sacrifice on the cross and for his perfect love. In** other words, we've learned the value of being a disciple and the treasure we have in following Jesus and serving him. To remind us of this valuable treasure, let's add gold trim to our flags.

Help kids cut and glue gold braid up the right sides of their flags. Then say: **Let's bow our heads as we hold our flags close and say a prayer thanking Jesus for his love and leadership.** Pray: **Dear Jesus, we're so proud to be your disciples! You have taught us how to love and serve others as we love and serve you, too. Thank you for loving us and for being the Lord and leader of our lives! Amen.**

If kids brought coins for the Find a Coin bank, have them donate their gifts at this time. Let kids know that you will be donating their coins to a local ministry or wherever kids decide they'd like their donations to go.

Say: **And now, for the last part of our flags—the flag pole!** Have kids slide the dowel rods inside the pockets on their flags, then wave them high. Say: **Now let's show everyone how proud we are to be Jesus' disciples. We'll march through church waving our flags and singing our marching song. We'll get others excited about being Jesus' disciples, too!**

After sharing your pride and enthusiasm with the church, march back to the room and close by saying: **Being a disciple doesn't end with our classtime; it goes on forever! Disciples never stop learning, loving, or serving Jesus! Wave your flags proudly, display them outside your homes, hang them in your rooms to tell everyone how happy you are to be disciple proud!**

End with this responsive good-bye:

Leader: **May you always grow as a disciple.**

Children: **And also you!**

Thank kids for coming and encourage them to hang their disciple flags where others can enjoy them and be reminded about the power and pride in being Jesus' disciples. Give each child a complete set of the Scripture strips and encourage kids to continue their growth as disciples by reviewing the verses they memorized.

PERFECT PROMISES

Isaiah 42:6, 7

_____

_____

_____

Micah 5:2, 4, 5

_____

_____

_____

_____

DISCIPLE ID CARDS

DISCIPLE PROUD!

This is to show that

_____

is a disciple of Jesus
and proud of it!

Expiration Date: <u>NEVER!</u>

DISCIPLE PROUD!

This is to show that

_____

is a disciple of Jesus
and proud of it!

Expiration Date: <u>NEVER!</u>

SUNGLASSES PATTERN

WHY, WHAT, HOW?

Read Mark 1:29-31; Luke 5:4-11; 17:11-19 to discover why these people needed Jesus' help, what Jesus did to help them, and how the people responded! Write your answers in the spaces.

Mark 1:29-31

WHY did the person need help?

WHAT did Jesus do to serve?

HOW did the person respond?

Luke 5:4-11

WHY did these people need help?

WHAT did Jesus do to serve?

HOW did these people respond?

Luke 17:11-19

WHY did these people need help?

WHAT did Jesus do to serve?

HOW did these people respond?

SCRIPTURE DOLLAR

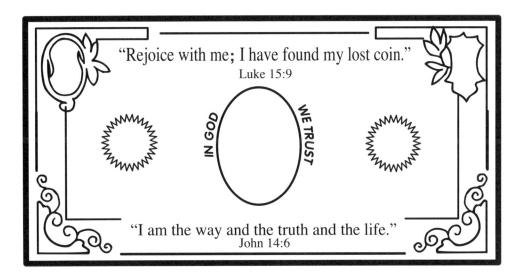

"Rejoice with me; I have found my lost coin."
Luke 15:9

IN GOD WE TRUST

"I am the way and the truth and the life."
John 14:6

TRAFFIC SIGNS

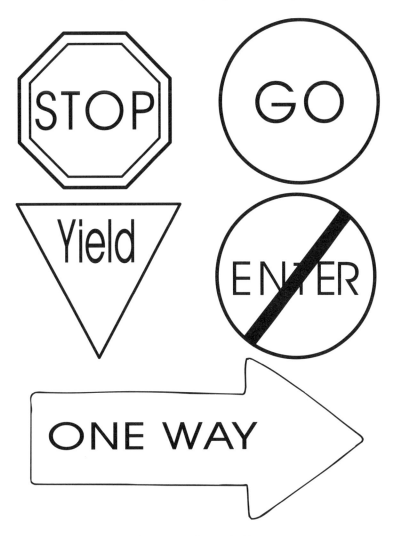

JOHN 3:16 REBUS PATTERNS

WOULD YOU CARDS

| **PEOPLE** | **THINGS** | **JESUS** |

| your family | a stranger across town | your possessions and toys | your favorite pet | all people in the world |

| your best friend | a robber in another country | your home | being able to see | his life |

SCRIPTURE STRIPS

We have seen and testify that the Father has sent his Son to be the Savior of the world. *1 John 4:14*

The Word became flesh and made his dwelling among us. *John 1:14a*

That at the name of Jesus every knee should bow, in heaven and on earth and under the earth, and every tongue confess that Jesus Christ is Lord, to the glory of God the Father. *Philippians 2:10, 11*

For the wages of sin is death, but the gift of God is eternal life in Christ Jesus our Lord. *Romans 6:23*

I am the way and the truth and the life. No one comes to the Father except through me. *John 14:6*

Whoever claims to live in him must walk as Jesus did. *1 John 2:6*

For God so loved the world that he gave his one and only Son, that whoever believes in him shall not perish but have eternal life. *John 3:16*

A new command I give you: Love one another. *John 13:34a*